Celebrating Language and Literacy for Infants, Toddlers & Twos

A User's Guide by
Jan Greenberg, Hilary Parrish,
and Candy Jones
Teaching Strategies, Inc.

DVD by
Joanne Knapp-Philo, Ph.D.
Sonoma State University
From the StoryQUEST Project

Teaching Strategies, Inc.
P.O. Box 42243
Washington, DC 20015
www.TeachingStrategies.com

ISBN: 978-1-933021-36-2

Teaching Strategies and *The Creative Curriculum* names and logos
are registered trademarks of Teaching Strategies, Inc.,
Washington, D.C.

Library of Congress Control Number: 2008923877

Printed and bound in the United States of America

2012	2011	2010	2009	2008
5	4	3	2	1

Table of Contents

Introduction

Planning the Training vii

Workshops for Staff Members and Families viii

Chapter 1: Celebrating Language and Literacy for Infants, Toddlers & Twos

Workshops for Staff Members 2

    Exploring Our Beliefs 4

    Everyday Language and Literacy Experiences 14

    Relationships Are Key 24

Chapter 2: Strategies for Early Language and Literacy Development

Workshop for Staff Members 33

    Introducing the Video to Staff Members: First Viewing 34

Chapter 3: Vocabulary and Language

Workshops for Staff Members 38

    Talking With Young Children 40

    Relationship-Based Turn-Taking 46

    Using Everyday Experiences, Routines, and Environments to Support Young Children's Language Development 58

Chapter 4: The Sounds and Rhythms of Language

Workshops for Staff Members 66

    The Sounds Around Us 68

    The Sounds of Songs 78

    Making Musical Instruments 84

Chapter 5: Exploring Writing

Workshops for Staff Members 88

    Learning About Symbols 90

    Viewing the Video: "Exploring Writing" 102

    Stages of Writing Development 110

Chapter 6: Enjoying Books and Stories

Workshops for Staff Members 120

    Telling Stories 122

    Viewing the Video: "Enjoying Stories and Books" 130

    Choosing Books for Infants, Toddlers, and Twos 136

    Making a Book 152

Handouts

For Staff Workshops:

1A .... Video Messages

1B .... Reflecting on the Video Messages

1C .... Reflecting on Video Messages From a Program's Point of View

1D .... How Materials and Activities Contribute to Language and Literacy Development

1E .... Making Everyday Experiences More Intentional and Meaningful

1F .... Supporting Language and Literacy Development Through Positive Relationships

1G .... Practicing What You Learned

2A .... A Viewing Guide for *Strategies for Early Language and Literacy Development*

3A .... Ideas, Ideas, Ideas

3B .... Relationship-Based Turn-Taking

3C .... Practicing Relationship-Based Turn-Taking

3D .... Your Turn, My Turn

3E .... Supporting Language Development Anytime, Anywhere

4A .... The Sounds of Language

4B .... Sounds on a Walk

4C .... Exploring Language and Literacy Through Songs, Chants, Rhymes, and Fingerplays

5A .... Strategies to Help Infants, Toddlers, and Twos Learn About Symbols and What They Mean

5B .... Symbols in the Community

5C .... Experiences With Print and Writing

5D .... Stages of Writing Development

5E .... Children's Scribbles and Drawings

5F .... Children's Scribbles and Drawings: Answer Key

6A .... Building a Story to Tell

6B .... Tips for Storytelling

6C .... "Enjoying Stories and Books": A Viewing Guide

6D .... Good Books for Infants, Toddlers, and Twos

6E .... Choosing Good Books for Infants, Toddlers, and Twos

6F .... General Tips for Reading and Storytelling With Children

6G .... More Tips for Enjoying Stories and Books With Infants, Toddlers, and Twos

6H .... Making Books for Children

For Family Workshops:

F1A .... Video Messages

F1B .... Reflecting on the Video Messages

F1C .... More Reflections

F1D .... How Activities Contribute to Language and Literacy Development

F1E .... Making Everyday Experiences More Meaningful

F1F .... Supporting Language and Literacy Development Through Positive Relationships

F1G .... Practicing What You Learned

F3A .... Ideas, Ideas, Ideas

F3B .... Relationship-Based Turn-Taking

F3C .... Practicing Relationship-Based Turn-Taking

F3D.............. Your Turn, My Turn

F3E .... Supporting Language Development Anytime, Anywhere

F4A .... The Sounds of Language

F4B .... Sounds on a Walk

F4C .... Exploring Language and Literacy Through Songs, Chants, Rhymes, and Fingerplays

F5A .... Strategies to Help Your Child Learn About Symbols and What They Mean

F5B .... Symbols in the Community

F5C .... Experiences With Print and Writing

F5D.............. What You Can Do at Home to Support Your Child's Experiences With Symbols and Writing

F5E .... Recipes for Playdough, Baker's Clay, and Goop

F5F .... Stages of Writing for Infants, Toddlers, and 2-Year-Olds

F5G .... Children's Scribbles and Drawings

F5H.............. Children's Scribbles and Drawings: Answer Key

F6A .... Building a Story to Tell

F6B .... Tips for Storytelling

F6C.............. "Enjoying Stories and Books": A Viewing Guide

F6D.............. Good Books for Infants, Toddlers, and 2-Year-Olds

F6E .... Choosing Books for Your Infant, Toddler, or 2-Year-Old

F6F .... Tips for Enjoying Stories and Books With Your Infant, Toddler, or 2-Year-Old

F6G .... Making Books for Children

Introduction

A *User's Guide* is designed to help you get the most out of two videos, *Celebrating Language and Literacy for Infants, Toddlers & Twos* and *Strategies for Early Language and Literacy Development*. The videos show adults how to support young children's language and literacy development through relationships and by making intentional use of daily routines and experiences in child care centers, in community settings, and at home. Both videos were developed originally for the StoryQUEST Project at Sonoma State University and are excellent companions for programs implementing *The Creative Curriculum®* *for Infants, Toddlers & Twos*. The videos and this user's guide, however, are a valuable training resource for any program that serves very young children and their families.

The first video, *Celebrating Language and Literacy for Infants, Toddlers & Twos*, is 11 minutes long. It provides an introduction to the development of early literacy skills within the context of caring relationships and children's experiences with families, teachers, and communities. Messages about early language and literacy are beautifully illustrated through video footage and the voices of children and adults. *Celebrating Language and Literacy for Infants, Toddlers & Twos* is ideal for sharing with families to help them think about how they can help their children develop language and literacy skills. Early childhood program staffs also will enjoy the video as an introduction to the language and literacy concepts that they will explore in more detail in the second video, *Strategies for Early Language and Literacy Development*.

Strategies for Early Language and Literacy Development (32 minutes) shows how everyday routines, experiences, and environments are tools that adults can use to help infants, toddlers, and twos learn. It also explains the importance of nurturing relationships; listening and talking; helping children discover the world through language and experiences; modeling literacy in everyday life; sounds in the environment; rhyme, rhythm, and songs; using symbols to communicate meaning; experiences with print and writing; and enjoying stories and books. The video features early childhood educators and parents who share best practices in language and literacy development. It is an ideal resource for in-service and pre-service training to build staff members' knowledge and skills and for family meetings and workshops on literacy topics.

A User's Guide offers general suggestions for planning and preparing for training and step-by-step instructions for workshops for early childhood program staff members and families of young children.

Planning the Training

Review the videos carefully so that you know the content well. This will help you focus participants' attention on the content that is most relevant to the specific workshop you are conducting. It will also prepare you to answer their questions.

Choose the workshops you want to present on the basis of following:

- what you know about the needs and interests of your group;
- the time you have available; and
- the content you have mastered and feel comfortable presenting.

The workshops have been designed to allow trainers maximum flexibility in planning and scheduling. Each workshop is a complete experience that can be offered alone or combined with other workshops during longer trainings. When multiple workshops are presented to the same participants, trainers have the option of beginning a workshop with a review of previously learned material.

Read the workshop descriptions and instructions carefully from start to finish as you prepare for the training. The workshop instructions will tell you what you need to do to prepare, such as gathering materials, copying handouts, or reviewing a video segment. Make sure that you have the proper equipment for viewing DVDs.

Some workshops require that you make collections of toys or books for participants to use. Others instruct trainers to prepare visual aids before the workshop, such as a list of questions to display. For brevity's sake, the workshop instructions refer to these visual aids as *charts*, but you also may use overhead transparencies or PowerPoint slides. If you choose charts, an easel will be helpful. If you choose transparencies or slides, you will need an overhead projector or a computer and LCD projector, and a space on which to project the transparency or slide.

Step-by-step instructions for the trainer are provided for each activity, with suggestions of what to tell and ask participants. This information appears in bullet form. Feel free to put the text into your own words and use the bullets as talking points.

To help you lead discussions, some activities include a list of possible responses to questions you will ask as part of the workshop. As you review the workshop instructions before the training, you may want to note possible responses to other questions as well. Prepare your own stories to share with workshop participants. Sharing personal stories is a powerful way to make people comfortable and more willing to share their experiences.

Adapt the activities and instructions to fit your situation and the needs of your participants. For example, if you have limited time, you can ask each group respond to one question on a handout rather than ask all of the groups to respond to every question. Whatever adaptations you make, be sure to allow enough time for participants to ask questions and share their ideas so that the workshop doesn't feel like a lecture.

Workshops for Staff Members and Families

A User's Guide offers the following workshops linked to the *Celebrating Literacy for Infants, Toddlers, and Twos* video for use with early childhood staff members:

- Exploring Our Beliefs
- Everyday Language and Literacy Experiences
- Relationships Are Key

Workshops linked to the *Strategies for Early Language and Literacy Development* video include the following:

- Introducing the Video to Staff Members: First Viewing

- Vocabulary and Language (includes nurturing relationships, listening and talking, discovering the world through words and experiences, and modeling literacy in everyday life)

    Talking With Young Children

    Relationship-Based Turn-Taking

    Using the Everyday Environment to Support Young Children's Language Development

- The Sounds and Rhythms of Language (includes environmental sounds, rhyme, rhythm, and song)

    The Sounds Around Us

    The Sounds of Songs

    Making Musical Instruments

- Exploring Writing (includes using symbols to communicate, and experiences with print and writing)

    Learning About Symbols

    Viewing the Video: Exploring Writing

    Stages of Writing Development

- Enjoying Stories and Books

    Telling Stories

    Viewing the Video: Enjoying Stories and Books

    Choosing Books for Infants, Toddlers, and Twos

    Making a Book

Adapting Workshops for Families

The workshops in the User's Guide, while geared toward teachers, can also be easily adapted for use with families. In addition to the general guidelines in the "Planning the Training" section, here are some additional things to consider:

General adaptations

- Suggestions about what things to tell and ask participants are written with a teacher focus. Think about how you would say the same things to families. Change program references to family-focused, family-friendly references. For example, say, "your child" or "how you interact with your child" rather than "infants, toddlers, and twos," "young children," "children in your room or group," or "program practices."

- Develop "possible responses" that family members are likely to say.

- For activities in which participants are grouped by age, invite them to form groups according to the ages of their children: infants, toddlers, or 2-year-olds.

- Educational terms that may be familiar to teachers may not be familiar to families. Use the terms during training but think about how you can define them in clear, understandable ways. For example, family members may not be familiar with the term *eye-hand coordination*. You might offer the following definition: using one's eyes to guide one's hands.

Specific adaptations

All the workshops for both videos except "Introducing the Video to Staff Members: First Viewing," include adaptations that are specific to the workshop. They can be found at the end of each section. These adaptations include talking points, handouts, alternate headings for activities using chart paper, additional workshop activities, and suggestions for taking the training home.

Celebrating Language and Literacy for Infants, Toddlers & Twos

Celebrating Language and Literacy for Infants, Toddlers & Twos shows how early literacy skills develop in the context of caring relationships and experiences with families, providers, and communities. It provides examples of the many ways that language and literacy develop in a variety of cultures and languages, and it demonstrates how adults can help very young children understand the world around them. These key messages are presented:

- Preparing children to read prepares children for life.

- It's never too early to give a baby a book.

- Every baby should be talked with and read to.

- Babbling is the beginning of speech.

- Scribbling is the beginning of script.

- Play is the work of childhood.

- Literacy thrives when children are nurtured by strong families empowered by high-quality services and supportive communities.

- Relationships are the heart of early language and literacy.

- Young children learn to "read" the world through experiences.

- There is a story in every language, language in every story.

Celebrating Language and Literacy for Infants, Toddlers & Twos

Workshops for Staff Members

WORKSHOP	KEY POINTS	MATERIALS	TIME (minutes)
Exploring Our Beliefs (p. 4)	Beliefs about supporting language and literacy learning for infants, toddlers, and twos affect program practices, so it is important to explore these beliefs. Understanding the importance of supporting young children's language and literacy development inspires you to make your practices more literacy focused.	☐ Chart paper ☐ Markers ☐ Tape ☐ Prepared chart ☐ Video messages in paper bag or basket ☐ DVD player and monitor, or computer and LCD projector ☐ *Celebrating Language and Literacy for Infants, Toddlers & Twos* video ☐ Handout 1A. Video Messages ☐ Handout 1B. Reflecting on the Video Messages ☐ Handout 1C: Reflecting on Video Messages From a Program's Point of View	60–75
Everyday Language and Literacy Experiences (p. 14)	Language and literacy are part of everyday experiences. You are already doing many things that support children's language and literacy development. However, you can also be more intentional about how you do this through daily activities and experiences.	☐ Chart paper ☐ Markers ☐ Tape ☐ Handout 1D. How Materials and Activities Contribute to Language and Literacy Development ☐ Handout 1E. Making Everyday Experiences More Intentional and Meaningful	75–90

WORKSHOP	KEY POINTS	MATERIALS	TIME (minutes)
Relationships Are Key (p. 24)	Adults play a key role in children's language and literacy development. Through relationships, adults get to know children as individuals and offer support that promotes language and literacy learning.	☐ Chart paper ☐ Markers ☐ Tape ☐ DVD player and monitor, or computer and LCD projector ☐ *Celebrating Language and Literacy for Infants, Toddlers & Twos* video ☐ Handout 1F. Supporting Language and Literacy Development Through Positive Relationships ☐ Handout 1G. Practicing What You Learned	60–75

Exploring Our Beliefs

Preparation

Prepare a chart with the following question:

- Is literacy possible for infants, toddlers, and twos?

Read Handout 1A, "Video Messages." Choose one of the messages as the one that you will ask all participants to reflect on. Cut the handout into strips with one message per strip, and put the strips into a paper bag or basket. Don't include the strip with the message you selected for the entire group.

Duplicate Handout 1B, "Reflecting on the Video Messages," and Handout 1C, "Reflecting on the Video Messages From a Program's Point of View."

Preview *Celebrating Language and Literacy for Infants, Toddlers & Twos.* It is about 11 minutes long.

Introduction

Introduce the workshop by posting the chart with the question. Ask participants to choose a partner and talk about the question with that person. Allow time for the pairs to talk. Then ask for volunteers to share their responses. As they share, make the following point:

- We have just been exploring our beliefs about supporting the language and literacy learning of infants, toddlers, and twos. Because what we believe about literacy affects what we do, it's a useful exercise to stop and explore our beliefs.

Activity

Prepare participants for viewing *Celebrating Language and Literacy for Infants, Toddlers & Twos.* Tell them:

- The video we are about to watch, *Celebrating Language and Literacy for Infants, Toddlers & Twos,* highlights the importance of early language and literacy. It is about 11 minutes long.

- Pay particular attention to the written messages.

- Write down any messages that grab your attention—because you agree or disagree—on Handout 1B, "Reflecting on the Video Messages."

□ Chart paper, markers, and tape
□ Prepared chart
□ Video messages in paper bag or basket
□ DVD player and monitor, or computer and LCD projector
□ *Celebrating Language and Literacy for Infants, Toddlers & Twos* video
□ Handout 1A
□ Handout 1B
□ Handout 1C

Show the video. Then tell participants:

- Take some time to reflect by yourself on two of the messages that you wrote down while you watched the video and on one message that I have chosen for everyone. This is my message: [chosen message].

- Use the questions on Handout 1B, "Reflecting on the Video Messages," to guide your thoughts. Take a few minutes and think about what you believe about the three messages.

Allow time for this individual reflection. Then ask participants to form small groups of 3–4 persons. Ask them to discuss the message you provided for the individual reflection exercise and to choose a second message from the bag or basket of messages. Then give the following directions:

- Now reflect on the messages from a program's point of view. Use the questions on Handout 1C, "Reflecting on the Video Messages from a Program's Point of View," to guide your thoughts. Ask one person in your group to be the recorder.

Allow time for group reflection. Then ask each group to share its thoughts about the messages and to highlight the points that stimulated the most discussion.

SUMMARY

Summarize the workshop by reinforcing the following points:

- It is important to explore your beliefs about supporting language and literacy learning for infants, toddlers, and twos, because what you believe affects your program practices.

- You can begin to evaluate your practices to see if they support the important ideas about language and literacy learning presented as the key messages.

Adapting the Workshop for Families

If you are presenting this workshop to families, consider the following adaptations:

- Use Handout F1A, "Video Messages," to cut into strips with one message per strip.

- Use Handout F1B, "Reflecting on the Video Messages," for the individual reflection activity. Review the questions with participants.

- Use Handout F1C, "More Reflections," for the group reflection activity. Review the questions with participants.

- In summarizing the workshop, make the following points:

   It is useful to explore your beliefs about supporting language and literacy learning for infants, toddlers, and twos because what you believe affects the way you interact with your child.

   It is also important to think about the ways you already help your child learn about language and literacy and to appreciate your role as your child's first and most important teacher.

Notes:

Handout 1A.
Video Messages

— —

Preparing children to read prepares children for life.

— —

It's never too early to give a baby a book.

— —

Every baby should be talked with and read to.

— —

Babbling is the beginning of speech.

— —

Scribbling is the beginning of script.

— —

Play is the work of childhood.

— —

Literacy thrives when children are nurtured by strong families empowered by high quality services and supportive communities.

— —

Relationships are the heart of early language and literacy.

— —

Young children learn to read the world through experiences.

— —

There is a story in every language, language in every story.

— —

Handout 1B.
Reflecting on the Video Messages

Questions to focus your reflections:

- What is your initial reaction to the message? Why?

- How does it make you feel?

- How does it relate to your experiences?

- What does the message mean to you?

- How does it affect the work you do?

Message 1: _____

Message 2: _____

Message 3: _____

Message from the trainer: _____

Handout 1C.
Reflecting on Video Messages From a Program's Point of View

Questions to focus your reflections:

- What does this message mean to you?

- Does it fit your program's philosophy? Why or why not?

- What are the implications of this message for programs, families, and communities? Are there cultural aspects that need to be considered?

- How does this message affect your work?

- What would your program look like if this message is believed and put into practice?

Message from the trainer: _____

Additional message: _____

Handout F1A.
Video Messages

- -

Preparing children to read prepares children for life.

- -

It's never too early to give a baby a book.

- -

Every baby should be talked with and read to.

- -

Babbling is the beginning of speech.

- -

Scribbling is the beginning of script.

- -

Play is the work of childhood.

- -

Literacy thrives when children are nurtured by strong families empowered by high quality services and supportive communities.

- -

Relationships are the heart of early language and literacy.

- -

Young children learn to read the world through experiences.

- -

There is a story in every language, language in every story.

- -

Handout F1B.
Reflecting on the Video Messages

Questions to focus your reflections:

- What is your initial reaction to the message? Why?

- How does it make you feel?

- How does it relate to your experiences?

- What does the message mean to you?

- How does it affect the way you interact with your child?

Message 1: _____

Message 2: _____

Message 3: _____

Message from the Trainer: _____

Handout F1C.
More Reflections

Questions to focus your reflections:

- What does this message mean to you?

- Does the message have a cultural aspect that needs to be considered?

- Have your beliefs about this message changed over time?

- Is this belief different from what you experienced as a child?

- Does your belief match the child care program's belief? How do you know?

- How does it affect the way you interact with your child?

Message from the trainer: _____

Additional message: _____

Everyday Language and Literacy Experiences

☐ Chart paper
☐ Markers
☐ Tape
☐ Handout 1D
☐ Handout 1E

Preparation

Prepare a chart with the following instructions: *Think of a favorite activity or hobby. Now take a moment to think of the language and literacy skills you use during that activity.*

Duplicate the two handouts.

Introduction

Introduce the workshop by making the following points:

- Language and literacy are part of everyday experiences.

- You can reflect on your current practices and determine how to make them more intentionally literacy focused.

Activity

Refer participants to the chart. Ask them to think of a favorite activity or hobby, take a few minutes to think of the language and literacy skills used during that activity, and write them down. If participants need an example, tell them the following:

- As an example, let's think about knitting. Knitting makes use of a variety of language and literacy skills:

  Read to learn about patterns.

  Learn the vocabulary of knitting.

  Write a list of knitting supplies to take to the knitting store.

  Watch, listen to, and follow the directions of others to learn different stitches.

Give participants a few minutes to write their answers. When they are finished, invite two or three to share their responses. Write them on chart paper and note the activity or hobby and the literacy skills involved.

Then tell the group:

- Let's brainstorm for a few minutes about the following question: What is literacy?

Write the responses on chart paper. Call attention to the different kinds of activities listed. Make the following points:

- Literacy involves more than reading. It also includes listening, speaking, and writing.

- To be literate means to be able to communicate effectively with others: to understand what others are saying orally or through written language and to be understood by others.

Continue brainstorming with a second question:

- What is literacy for infants, toddlers, and twos? Is it different? What is the focus?

Write the responses on chart paper. Then make the following points:

- Early literacy is what young children know about reading and writing before they can do those things. It includes experiences children have with language, print, and books from the time they are born.

- It is important to recognize what emerging literacy behaviors for infants, toddlers, and twos look like. For example, smiling back at a smiling face, cooing and babbling, chewing on the pages of a board book, using gestures like pointing and nodding, looking at pictures in books, and using one thing to represent something else (like a block as a telephone), are all literacy behaviors.

- Young children develop language and literacy skills through their interactions with adults during daily routines and activities.

- We can turn almost any daily routine or activity into a literacy activity by paying attention to and emphasizing its language and literacy aspects.

Tell participants they will now look at how the daily activities of infants and toddlers include or lead to the development of language and literacy skills.

Ask participants to form groups of 3–4 persons. Give each group a piece of chart paper and ask them to fold it in half lengthwise to form two columns. Have them write on the top left of the paper "Material and Activity" and on the top right "What the Child Is Doing That Contributes to Language and Literacy Development."

Ask each person in the group to name one or two materials or activities that are favorites of the children in their room and that are not normally thought of as language or literacy materials or activities. Ask them to list their responses on the left side of the chart paper. Participants also can complete Handout 1D, "How Materials and Activities Contribute to Language and Literacy Development," so that they have the information for later use.

Then invite the group to discuss how each material or activity contributes to children's language and literacy development and learning and to record their responses in the second column.

Possible responses:

Material and Activity	What the Child Is Doing That Contributes to Language and Literacy Development
Shaking a rattle	Developing eye-hand coordination, which is important for writing; learning to listen for a particular sound, which is a precursor to phonological awareness; learning new vocabulary
Playing peek-a-boo	Learning to think about something that is out of sight; engaging in the give and take of relating to others
Painting at an easel or with fingers	Developing the fine motor skills and eye-hand coordination that are necessary for writing; beginning to communicate ideas
Pretending to talk on the telephone or using another object for a telephone	Building oral language and vocabulary; learning about conversation; learning that an object can be a symbol, as a child later learns that letters symbolize sounds and words symbolize ideas
Playing with a shape sorter	Discriminating between shapes, which leads to later letter discrimination; building vocabulary for naming; building the eye-hand coordination skills and fine motor skills that are necessary for writing
Singing a familiar song	Learning new words in a fun, meaningful way; hearing and discriminating the sounds of language

As the groups complete their charts, ask them to post the charts on the wall. Invite participants to walk about, look at each of the charts, and add ideas that support how a material or activity contributes to literacy.

Debrief with the whole group. Ask participants what they notice about the charts. Highlight the following points:

- Language and literacy development begin early in life.

- You are already doing many things that support children's language and literacy development.

- Most everyday activities involve some aspect of language and literacy. The materials and activities you provide for children help them to:

    Learn new words and learn about the world around them, developing concepts for communicating orally and learning to read.

    Develop the fine motor and eye-hand coordination skills that are important for writing.

    Become aware of the sounds around them, the first step toward phonological awareness. Phonological awareness is the ability to hear the small units of sound in spoken language, such as hearing the syllables in their names (*Car-la*, *Jo-na-than*), words that rhyme (*cat*, *bat*), and the sounds of individual letters (/p/ in *Papa*).

Ask participants to discuss in pairs how they can be more deliberate or *intentional* about focusing on language and literacy with two of the activities or materials listed on their chart. Distribute and review Handout 1E, "Making Everyday Experiences More Intentional and Meaningful," and invite them to record their answers. Ask for volunteers to share their responses.

Summary

Summarize the workshop by reinforcing the following points:

- Language and literacy are part of everyday experiences.

- You are already doing many things that support children's language and literacy development.

- You can be more intentional about how you support language and literacy development through everyday activities and experiences.

Adapting the Workshop for Families

If you are presenting this workshop to families, consider the following adaptations:

- Prepare a chart with the following instructions: *What do you think of when you hear the words* language *and* literacy? *Write your ideas on an index card.* This will be used in the first activity in the workshop.

- Include the following point as you introduce the workshop:

  You can think about how you help your child develop language and literacy skills through everyday experiences and make those experiences even more focused on language and literacy.

- For the first workshop activity, refer participants to the question on the chart. Give them a few minutes to write their responses. When they are finished, invite volunteers to share what they wrote. Write their responses on chart paper. Emphasize that their responses are examples of listening, speaking, reading, and writing, which are parts of language and literacy.

- Continue the workshop with the next activity (think of a favorite activity or hobby and the language and literacy skills used in that activity).

- For the small-group activity using chart paper, ask participants to label the left column, "Favorite Activity to Do With Our Child" and the right column, "What Our Child Is Doing That Contributes to Language and Literacy Development." Ask each person in the group to name one or two favorite activities to do with their child and list them on the left side of the chart. Participants can also complete Handout F1D, "How Activities Contribute to Language and Literacy Development," so that they have the information for later use.

- Distribute and review Handout F1E, "Making Everyday Experiences More Meaningful," and invite participants to write their answers. Ask for volunteers to share their responses.

Notes:

Handout 1D.
How Materials and Activities Contribute to Language and Literacy Development

Material and Activity	What the Child Is Doing That Contributes to Language and Literacy Development

Handout 1E.
Making Everyday Experiences More Intentional and Meaningful

Material and Activity 1:_____

What will you do differently?

What literacy skill(s) will it support?

Where will this be included on your weekly planning form or other planning tool?

What kind of support do you need to implement your idea (for example, more information, additional materials, or someone who can model a technique for you)?

Material and Activity 2: _____

What will you do differently?

What literacy skill(s) will it support?

Where will this be included on your weekly planning form or other planning tool?

What kind of support do you need to implement your idea (for example, more information, additional materials, or someone who can model a technique for you)?

Handout F1D.
How Activities Contribute to Language and Literacy Development

Favorite Activity With Our Child	What Our Child Is Doing That Contributes to Language and Literacy Development

Handout F1E.
Making Everyday Experiences More Meaningful

Activity 1: _____

What will you do differently?

What literacy skill(s) will it support?

What kind of support do you need to try your idea (for example, more information, additional materials, or someone who can model a technique for you)?

Activity 2: _____

What will you do differently?

What literacy skill(s) will it support?

What kind of support do you need to try your idea (for example, more information, additional materials, or someone who can model a technique for you)?

Relationships Are Key

- [ ] Chart paper
- [ ] Markers
- [ ] Tape
- [ ] DVD player and monitor, or computer and LCD projector
- [ ] *Celebrating Language and Literacy for Infants, Toddlers & Twos* video
- [ ] Handout 1F
- [ ] Handout 1G

Preparation

Prepare and post a chart with the following: *Think of a positive literacy experience from your childhood. Turn to a partner and share the experience and why it was positive.*

Prepare one chart for each table with the following headings:

- Adult-Child Interaction
- What Makes It A Positive Relationship?
- How and Why It Supports Language and Literacy Development

Duplicate the two handouts.

Introduction

Introduce the workshop by making the following points:

- Relationships are key to helping infants, toddlers, and twos develop language and literacy skills.
- You can strengthen your relationships with children and make your interactions with them even more literacy focused.

Activity

Refer participants to the posted chart. Ask them to think of a positive literacy experience from their childhood and turn to a partner and share that experience and why it was positive.

Prepare participants for viewing the *Celebrating Language and Literacy for Infants, Toddlers & Twos* video. If these participants have taken part in the "Exploring Our Beliefs" workshop, remind them that, when they watched the video before, they focused on the messages in the video. Invite them to watch it this time with a different focus: relationships.

Tell participants:

- Pay particular attention to the relationships you see throughout the video.
- Note on the left-hand column of Handout 1F, "Supporting Language and Literacy Development Through Positive Relationships," any adult-child interaction that demonstrates a positive relationship.

Show the video. Then, ask participants to work in pairs and share the adult-child interactions that they noticed. Give them the following directions:

- As you share each interaction, discuss what was happening that helped you know it was a positive relationship. Why and how is that interaction important to language and literacy development?

- Complete the middle and right-hand columns of Handout 1F, "Supporting Language and Literacy Development Through Positive Relationships."

- Once the handout is complete, decide as a pair on one interaction that shows a positive adult-child relationship and supports language and literacy development. Write it on the chart paper that I've given your table.

- Once all pairs at your table have written their interaction on the chart, ask someone in your group to post the chart on the wall.

Allow enough time for everyone to complete the activity and post the charts on the wall. Debrief by leading a discussion with the whole group on two or three of the posted interactions. Ask participants to talk about how they know the relationship is a positive one and how it supports the language and literacy development of infants, toddlers, and twos. Highlight the following points:

- Adults play a key role in children's language and literacy development.

- Through relationships, adults get to know children as individuals and offer support that promotes language and literacy learning.

- The adult's role is varied and ever changing. Adults play, model, encourage, validate, and nurture. They also are resources who provide materials, words, and information about the world.

- All adults—family members, teachers, other early childhood staff members, and community members—have many opportunities to promote children's language and literacy learning.

Invite participants to choose one thing they want to do strengthen their relationship with a child or more children in their group and enhance language and literacy development. Explain that they can tie this to an everyday experience they are working on from a previous workshop or a new everyday experience. Ask participants to write their plans on Handout 1G, "Practicing What You Learned." Invite two or three participants to share their plans.

Summary

Summarize the workshop by reinforcing the following points:

- Relationships are key to helping infants, toddlers, and twos develop language and literacy skills.

- You can be more intentional about supporting children's language and literacy development through your interactions and relationships with children.

Adapting the Workshop for Families

If you are presenting this workshop to families, consider the following adaptations:

- Use Handout F1F, "Supporting Language and Literacy Development Through Positive Relationships."

- For the last activity of the workshop, invite participants to choose one thing they want to do to strengthen their relationship with their child and enhance his or her language and literacy development. Explain that they can tie this to an everyday experience they are working on from the last session or a new everyday routine or experience. Participants may write their ideas on Handout F1G, "Practicing What You Learned."

Notes:

Handout 1F.
Supporting Language and Literacy Development Through Positive Relationships

Adult-Child Interaction	What Makes It a Positive Relationship	How and Why It Supports Language and Literacy Development

Handout 1G.
Practicing What You Learned

How are you going to strengthen your relationships with a child or children to enhance language and literacy development?

What everyday experience(s) are you going to link it to?

What kind of support do you need to implement your ideas?

How will you make sure that you are consistently implementing your ideas?

Handout F1F.
Supporting Language and Literacy Development Through Positive Relationships

Adult-Child Interaction	What Makes It A Positive Relationship	How and Why It Supports Language and Literacy Development

Handout F1G.
Practicing What You Learned

How are you going to strengthen your relationship with your child to support his or her language and literacy development?

What everyday experience(s) or routine(s) are you going to link it to?

What kind of support do you need to try your ideas (for example, more information; someone who can model a technique for you)?

Strategies for Early Language and Literacy Development

Workshop For Staff Members

Workshop	Key Points	Materials	Time (minutes)
Introducing the Video to Staff Members: First Viewing (p. 34)	Infants, toddlers, and twos need intentional experiences every day so they can acquire the building blocks of language and literacy. These include experiences that enable children to acquire vocabulary and language skills, hear the different sounds and rhythms of language, explore writing, and enjoy stories and books.	☐ Chart paper ☐ Markers ☐ Tape ☐ Collection of differently colored pens ☐ DVD player and monitor, or computer and LCD projector ☐ *Strategies for Early Language and Literacy Development* video ☐ Handout 2A. A Viewing Guide for *Strategies for Early Language and Literacy Development*	60–75

WORKSHOP

Introducing the Video to Staff Members: First Viewing

Handout 2A.
A Viewing Guide for *Strategies for Early Language and Literacy Development*

Vocabulary and Language (nurturing relationships, listening and talking, discovering the world through words and experiences, modeling the purposes of literacy)
What I do now:

Surprises, ideas, insights:

Sounds (environmental sounds, rhyme, rhythm, and song)
What I do now:

Surprises, ideas, insights:

Exploring Writing (using symbols to communicate, and experiences with print and writing)
What I do now:

Surprises, ideas, insights:

Enjoying Stories and Books
What I do now:

Surprises, ideas, insights:

☐ Chart paper
☐ Marker
☐ Tape
☐ Collection of differently colored pens
☐ DVD player and monitor, or computer and LCD projector
☐ *Strategies for Early Language and Literacy Development* video
☐ Handout 2A

Preparation

As a rule, participants will get more out of a first viewing of *Strategies for Early Language and Literacy Development* if you provide them with a focus. This activity provides that focus.

Put a collection of differently colored pens on each table. Make sure there are enough pens so that each participant can write with two different colors.

Copy the handout.

Introduction

Introduce the workshop by making the following points:

- A baby's brain is primed for acquiring language.

- When young children are around caring and responsive adults who engage them in conversations, read and tell stories to them every day, and teach them songs and rhymes, they are eager to communicate.

- Because infants, toddlers, and twos are very motivated to engage with others and communicate, your responsive interactions with them can make a positive difference that will last a lifetime.

- Infants, toddlers, and twos need you intentionally to offer experiences every day so that they can acquire the building blocks of language and literacy. These include experiences that help children acquire vocabulary and language skills, hear the different sounds and rhythms of language, explore writing, and enjoy stories and books.

Activity

Distribute Handout 2A, "A Viewing Guide for *Strategies for Early Language and Literacy Development.*" Instruct participants:

- Look at your viewing guide handout and complete the "What I Do Now" section for each topic that we are going to learn about in the video. Use one of the colored pens on your table.

Allow time for participants to complete the task. Then debrief with the group. Go through each category on the handout, asking volunteers to share their current language and literacy practices and activities.

Prepare participants for viewing the *Strategies for Early Language and Literacy Development* video by telling them:

- The video we are going to see shows how adults can use everyday routines, experiences, and environments to help infants, toddlers, and twos develop a strong foundation for later learning. It is about 32 minutes long.

- As you watch the video, jot down information, practices, and activities you see that surprise you or give you new ideas or insights for supporting young children's language and literacy development. Use the "Surprises, Ideas, and Insights" section of your viewing guide handout.

- Use a different color to note your surprises, ideas, and insights.

Show the video. When it is over, debrief with the group. Ask participants to share their surprises, ideas, and insights. Write their responses on chart paper. As participants share, reinforce the following points:

- For very young children, learning depends on the trusting relationships they build with the important adults in their lives.

- When children know they are safe, loved, and cared for, they are ready to venture out to explore everything around them. When adults encourage these explorations and share children's excitement about new discoveries, children gain confidence in themselves as learners.

- Almost everything you need to support young children's language and literacy development can be found in your everyday environment, routines, activities, and interactions.

- Young children's primary and most important relationships are with their families. It is important to understand and support families' language and literacy practices and to connect what happens in your program with what happens in children's homes and communities.

Summary

Let participants know that they will have opportunities to learn more about effective language and literacy practices and activities through additional workshops that focus on vocabulary and language, sounds, exploring writing, and enjoying stories and books.

Handout 2A.
A Viewing Guide for *Strategies for*
Early Language and Literacy Development

Vocabulary and Language (nurturing relationships, listening and talking, discovering the world through words and experiences, modeling the purposes of literacy)

What I do now:

Surprises, ideas, insights:

Sounds (environmental sounds, rhyme, rhythm, and song)

What I do now:

Surprises, ideas, insights:

Exploring Writing (using symbols to communicate, and experiences with print and writing)

What I do now:

Surprises, ideas, insights:

Enjoying Stories and Books

What I do now:

Surprises, ideas, insights:

Vocabulary and Language

Workshops For Staff Members

Workshop	Key Points	Materials	Time (minutes)
Talking With Young Children (p. 40)	Children explore language from the day they are born. This learning is supported by caring adults who respond to each attempt at communication and engage children in meaningful interactions. Adults who talk with children, describe things, reassure them, sing to them, and respond to their needs help build a strong foundation for future language and literacy learning.	☐ Chart paper ☐ Markers ☐ DVD player and monitor, or computer and LCD projector ☐ *Strategies for Early Language and Literacy Development* video ☐ Handout 3A. Ideas, Ideas, Ideas	60
Relationship-Based Turn-Taking (p. 46)	Relationship-based turn-taking helps infants, toddlers, and twos begin to understand the world and develop language and literacy skills. It can also help build caring relationships with young children.	☐ Collection of toys for infants, toddlers, and twos ☐ Handout 3B. Relationship-Based Turn-Taking ☐ Handout 3C. Practicing Relationship-Based Turn-Taking ☐ Handout 3D. Your Turn, My Turn	60

Workshop	Key Points	Materials	Time (minutes)
Using Everyday Experiences, Routines, and Environments to Support Young Children's Language Development (p. 58)	Every experience, routine, and environment has language development opportunities. Infants, toddlers, and twos hear and learn to use a lot of language when adults take advantage of the many opportunities that are available every day and everywhere for supporting their language development.	☐ Prepared chart ☐ DVD player and monitor, or computer and LCD projector ☐ *Strategies for Early Language and Literacy Development* video ☐ Handout 3E. Supporting Language Development Anytime, Anywhere	90

WORKSHOP

Talking With Young Children

Preparation

Post blank chart paper for the first activity.

Preview the "Vocabulary and Language" segment of the *Strategies for Early Language and Literacy Development* video.

Duplicate the handout.

Optional:

Review the following material in *The Creative Curriculum® for Infants, Toddlers & Twos*:

- "Vocabulary and Language," pages 110–113
- "Building Trusting Relationships," pages 138–140

Introduction

Introduce the workshop by making the following point:

- Children learn to understand the world—to make sense of what they see and hear—by watching and listening to adults.

Ask participants:

- What might children learn by watching and listening to adults?

Possible responses:

   What facial expressions mean

   Whether an activity is fun, scary, or boring

   When to use an inside or outside voice

   Reading is fun

Tell participants:

- Children explore language from the day they are born. This learning is supported by caring adults who respond to each attempt at communication and engage the children in meaningful interactions.

- Adults who talk with children, describe things, reassure them, sing to them, and respond to their needs help build a strong foundation for future language and literacy learning.

Materials checklist:

- ☐ Chart paper
- ☐ Markers
- ☐ Tape
- ☐ DVD player and monitor, or computer and LCD projector
- ☐ *Strategies for Early Language and Literacy Development* video
- ☐ Handout 3A

Activity

Make the following statement:

- Talking with young children is important.

Then ask participants why it is important to talk with children. Invite them to share their ideas. Record their responses on chart paper.

> ### Possible responses:
> *Build their vocabulary*
>
> *Learn their home language*
>
> *Help them express feelings*
>
> *Teach them what to do and what not to do*
>
> *Support their future literacy skills*
>
> *Build relationships*

As participants share their ideas, point out the following:

- Language experiences in the first 3 years of life affect language and literacy development greatly.

- The size of a child's vocabulary matters! The more words a child knows, the more she understands when someone reads to her and the more she will understand when she learns to read, herself.

- Young children who hear a lot of conversation and who are encouraged to talk have an easier time learning to read than children who hear little conversation and are not encouraged to talk.

Tell participants:

- Think about how you can enhance young children's language development. There are three main ideas to consider when talking with children:

  Make sure the experience or activity you are talking about is developmentally appropriate. It should match the children's interests and not be too easy or too hard for them.

  Follow the child's lead.

  Share the moment. Let the child know you are paying attention, listening, and responding to what he is saying or doing at that moment.

Ask participants to form groups of 3–4 persons. Then prompt,

- In your small groups, talk about each of the three ideas to think about when talking with children. Use Handout 3A, "Ideas, Ideas, Ideas," to guide your thinking.

Allow enough time for the groups to discuss the ideas.

Debrief by inviting groups to share their response to one of the ideas. Ask participants to consider how they can change their interactions when talking with children and invite them to share their thoughts.

Trainer's Note: If you have a small number of groups, ask each to share its discussion of more than one of the ideas. If you have a large number of groups, have more than one group share responses to the same idea.

Ask participants:

- Have you heard the term *parentese*? It is a way of talking to very young children that helps them learn the sounds of language. The characteristics of parentese include the following:

    Using a higher pitched, "sing-song" voice

    Exaggerating your facial expressions and the sounds in words you use

    Repeating words and phrases over and over

Continue the discussion about parentese with the following points:

- When you talk to infants in parentese:

    Use short, simple sentences and speak more slowly.

    Repeat what the child says to you.

    Pause between words.

    Talk about the here and now.

    Use a lot of questions and requests.

    Talk about objects the child is focused on or what the child is doing.

- Most families across cultures use these strategies to get their babies' attention.

Prepare participants for watching the "Vocabulary and Language" segment of the *Strategies for Early Language and Literacy Development* video. Tell them:

- As you watch the video, listen for messages about the importance of talking with children.

Show the video. When it is over, ask participants to share what they saw and heard about why it is important to talk with children. Let participants know that they might be watching this video section again in another workshop but with a different focus.

Taking The Training Home

Invite participants to take the training home. Suggest that they try the following:

- Keep a diary for a day on one child in your group. Note the following:

   Experiences in which the child engaged

   How and when you followed his lead

   How and when you shared moments

   How you supported his language and literacy development

- Look at your diary and review what you wrote on your "Ideas, Ideas, Ideas" handout. Ask yourself:

   Were the activities and experiences developmentally appropriate?

   Did I always follow the child's lead? If no, why not?

   Did I make the most of each moment I shared with her? If no, why not?

   Did I find ways and time throughout the day to support her language and literacy development?

   What worked well? What can I do differently?

- Expand your practice to include all the children in your group! Pay attention to planning developmentally appropriate experiences, following children's leads, making the most of shared moments, and supporting each child's language and literacy development.

Adapting the Workshop for Families

If you are presenting this workshop to families, consider the following adaptation:

- Use Handout F3A, "Ideas, Ideas, Ideas."

- In "Taking the Training Home," suggest the following:

   Keep talking to your child. Notice what you talk about, what words you use, and how you talk to your child, including whether you are using *parentese*.

   Follow your child's lead. Pay attention to how your child responds. That will help you know how to respond and keep the interaction going.

   Share moments with your child. Notice how your child—and you—respond to the interaction. Sharing moments helps your child learn that what he says and does is important to you.

Handout 3A.
Ideas, Ideas, Ideas

Offer developmentally appropriate experiences.

What are some appropriate experiences for children at these ages?

Young Infants (Birth–9 Months)   Mobile Infants (8–18 Months)

Toddlers (16–25 Months)   Twos (24–36 Months)

Follow the child's lead.

What are some things you do to ensure that you are following the child's lead?

Share the moment.

What does the phrase *share the moment with the child* mean to you? What do you do?

Handout F3A.
Ideas, Ideas, Ideas

Offer developmentally appropriate experiences
What are some appropriate experiences for children at these ages?

Young Infants (Birth-9 Months)   Mobile Infants (8-18 Months)

Toddlers (16-25 Months)   Twos (24-36 Months)

Follow your child's lead.
What are some things you do to ensure that you are following your child's lead?

Share the moment.
What does the phrase *share the moment with your child* mean to you? What do you do?

WORKSHOP

Relationship-Based Turn-Taking

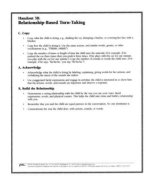

- ☐ Collection of toys for infants, toddlers, and twos
- ☐ Handout 3B
- ☐ Handout 3C
- ☐ Handout 3D

Preparation

Collect a variety of toys used in infant, toddler, and twos rooms. You need at least one toy for every three participants. Put the toys on a table in the training room.

Duplicate the three handouts.

Optional:

Review the following material in *The Creative Curriculum® for Infants, Toddlers & Twos*:

- "Vocabulary and Language," pages 110–113
- "Building Trusting Relationships," pages 138–140

Introduction

Introduce the workshop by making the following points:

- Humans are born into and learn through relationships.
- Young children thrive when they have close, supportive, and trusting relationships with the adults in their lives.
- When young children are around caring and responsive adults who talk with them and engage them in conversations, they are eager to communicate.

Activity

Trainer's Note: If the participants have taken part in the "Talking to Children" workshop, begin the activity by asking them to share their 1-day diary experiences. Ask them if they have noticed any changes in their interactions with children since the workshop.

Tell participants:

- The purpose of this workshop is to explore relationship-based turn-taking.
- Relationship-based turn-taking helps infants, toddlers, and twos begin to understand the world and to develop language and literacy skills.
- Turn-taking involves taking turns with a child (your turn, my turn; your turn, my turn). When you do this, you are following the child's lead while also being a good language model.

- The turns can include actions, such as clapping hands, or talking, such as repeating a word or sound. The turn-taking can occur quickly or slowly, and it can take place during experiences such as peek-a-boo or playing with toys.

- You can use the "CAB" technique to engage in relationship-based turn-taking with young children:

  Copy

  Acknowledge

  Build the relationship

Distribute and review Handout 3B, "Relationship-Based Turn-Taking." Invite participants to share examples from their own experiences and ask questions during the review. Make the following points for each feature:

- For C, Copy:

  You can quickly get a young child's attention when you copy what the child is doing.

  You can copy anything a child does or says: rolling a ball, opening and closing his mouth, looking at a book, laughing, shaking a rattle, saying *mama*, or filling a container with shapes.

  The goal is for you and the child to take turns, back and forth, back and forth. You want to have a conversational interaction.

- For A, Acknowledge:

  The goal is to keep the child engaged in the interaction.

  Acknowledge the child's actions and sounds, even if you are not sure what they mean. In other words, it is okay to interpret what you see and hear. The important point is to help the child learn that what he does and says matters to you.

- For B, Build the Relationship:

  You can communicate and build a positive relationship with a child through your tone of voice, facial expressions, physical contact, and words.

  Children will engage in turn-taking when they sense that you care about them.

Tell participants they will now have an opportunity to practice relationship-based turn-taking. Ask them to break into groups of three.

Distribute Handout 3C, "Practicing Relationship-Based Turn-Taking," and explain the following:

- Each person in the group will have an opportunity to be an observer; an infant, toddler, or 2-year-old; and an adult.

- The "child" will select a toy from the table.

- The "child" will play with the toy, and the adult will take turns to try to expand the interaction.

- The observer will watch the interaction and record what the adult did to prolong or end the interaction.

- Use the "Relationship-Based Turn-Taking" handout to help you evaluate the interaction. After each round, record your thoughts about the experience on the handout.

Once every participant has had a chance to engage in all three roles, provide time for the groups to talk about their experiences in each role. Then lead a whole-group discussion about the experience. To guide the discussion, ask participants:

- What did you notice when you were the child? How did it make you feel? How did the turn-taking help you?

- What was it like to engage in turn-taking as the adult? How did you feel? What was the easiest part? The most challenging part?

- What did you notice about the interaction when you were the observer?

- Did all three persons in your group have the same experience in each role? How was it the same? How was it different?

As participants share, highlight the following about turn-taking:

- It is the foundation for developing later conversation skills.

- It provides an opportunity for you to be a good language model.

- It keeps children engaged and keeps the interaction going.

- It is a way to show children that you care about what they do and say and to strengthen your relationship with them.

- It should be done in the context of play for both the child and adult.

End the workshop by reminding participants that relationships are the context in which language and literacy learning occur and that turn-taking is one way to build strong relationships with young children.

Taking The Training Home

Distribute Handout 3D, "Your Turn, My Turn," and invite participants to take the training home. Suggest that they try the following:

- Choose three children with whom to take turns during the same routine or experience, or choose one child with whom to interact during three different routines or experiences. Use the "Your Turn, My Turn" handout and record the turn-taking interactions. Think about what you learn from each interaction. Compare the interactions. What differences do you notice among the interactions?

- Keep practicing!

Adapting the Workshop for Families

If you are presenting this workshop to families, consider the following adaptations:

- In Trainer's Note: If participants have taken part in the "Talking With Children" workshop, begin the activity by asking them to share any changes they have made in the way they communicate with their child.

- Distribute and review Handout F3B, "Relationship-Based Turn-Taking" with participants in preparation for the turn-taking activity.

- Distribute Handout F3C, "Practicing Relationship-Based Turn-Taking" and explain the rules of the activity. Tell participants to use Handout F3B to help them evaluate the interaction.

- In "Taking the Training Home," distribute Handout F3D, "Your Turn, My Turn" and suggest the following:

    Try relationship-based turn-taking with your child. Use the "Your Turn, My Turn" handout to help you keep track of the experience. You can fill it out or use it as a reference. There are spaces to record three turn-taking interactions.

    Keep taking turns as you play with your child!

Handout 3B.
Relationship-Based Turn-Taking

C, Copy

- Copy *what* the child is doing, e.g., shaking the toy, dumping a bucket, or covering her face with a blanket.

- Copy *how* the child is doing it. Use the same actions, and similar words, grunts, or other vocalizations (e.g., "Ohhhh, ohhhh").

- Copy the number of times or length of time the child uses the material. (For example, if he pushed the car three times then you push it three times. If he plays with the car for one minute, you play with the car for one minute.) Copy the number of sounds or words the child uses. (For example, if he says, "Ba-ba-ba," you say, "Ba-ba-ba.").

A, Acknowledge

- Acknowledge what the child is doing by labeling, explaining, giving words for her actions, and verbalizing the intent of the sounds she makes.

- Use exaggerated facial expressions and engage in activities the child is interested in to show him that his actions, words, and sounds are important and deserve a response.

B, Build the Relationship

- Demonstrate a caring relationship with the child by the way you use your voice, facial expressions, words, and physical contact. This helps the child take turns and build a relationship with you.

- Remember that you and the child are equal partners in the conversation. No one dominates it.

- Communicate the way the child does, with actions, sounds, or words.

Handout 3C.
Practicing Relationship-Based Turn-Taking

Round One

Toy used in turn-taking interaction:

The infant, toddler, or 2-year-old…

The adult…

The observer…

Round Two

Toy used in turn-taking interaction:

The infant, toddler, or 2-year-old…

The adult…

The observer…

Round Three

Toy used in turn-taking interaction:

The infant, toddler, or 2-year-old…

The adult…

The observer…

Handout 3D.
Your Turn, My Turn

Routine or Experience	Turn-Taking Feature	Child's Response	Length of Interaction	Language and Literacy Skills and Additional Observations

Handout F3B.
Relationship-Based Turn-Taking

C, Copy

- Copy *what* your child is doing e.g., shaking the toy, dumping a bucket, or covering her face with a blanket.

- Copy *how* your child is doing it. Use the same actions and similar words, grunts, or other vocalizations e.g., ("Ohhhh, ohhhh").

- Copy the number of times or length of time that your child uses the material. (For example, if she pushed the car three times, then you push it three times. If she plays with the car for one minute, you play with the car for one minute.) Copy the number of sounds or words the child uses. (For example, if she says, "Ba-ba-ba," you say, "Ba-ba-ba.").

A, Acknowledge

- Acknowledge what your child is doing by labeling, explaining, giving words for his actions and verbalizing the intent of the sounds he makes.

- Use exaggerated facial expressions and engage in activities your child is interested in to show her that her actions, words, and sounds are important and deserve a response.

B, Build the Relationship

- Strengthen your relationship with your child by the way you use your voice, facial expressions, words, and physical contact. This helps your child take turns and strengthens his relationship with you.

- Remember that you and your child are equal partners in the conversation. No one dominates it.

- Communicate the way your child does, with actions, sounds, or words.

Handout F3C.
Practicing Relationship-Based Turn-Taking

Round One

Toy used in turn-taking interaction:

The infant, toddler, or 2-year-old...

The adult...

The observer...

Round Two

Toy used in turn-taking interaction:

The infant, toddler, or 2-year-old...

The adult...

The observer...

Round Three

Toy used in turn-taking interaction:

The infant/toddler/2-year-old...

The adult...

The observer...

Handout F3D.
Your Turn, My Turn

Routine or Experience	Turn-Taking Feature	My Child's Response	Length of Interaction	Language and Literacy Skills and Additional Observations

WORKSHOP

Using Everyday Experiences, Routines, and Environments to Support Young Children's Language Development

☐ Prepared chart

☐ DVD player and
    monitor, or computer
    and LCD projector

☐ *Strategies for Early
    Language and Literacy
    Development* video

☐ Handout 3E

Preparation

Preview the "Vocabulary and Language" segment of the *Strategies for Early Language and Literacy Development* video.

Duplicate the handout.

Optional:

Create a chart with the following questions:

- What did you notice about the child when you engaged in relationship-based turn-taking?

- What was the experience like for you as the adult?

- What was positive about using the techniques? What was challenging about using the techniques?

Ask participants in advance to bring their completed "Your Turn, My Turn" handout.

Optional:

Review the following material in *The Creative Curriculum® for Infants, Toddlers & Twos*:

- "Vocabulary and Language," pages 110–113

- "What You Can Do and Say," page 119

- "Part 2: Routines," 219–287

- "Part 3: Experiences," pages 289–421

Introduction

Introduce the activity by making the following points:

- From the time children say their first word around their first birthday until they are about 3-years old, children learn words at an astounding rate and how to put them together.

- Children's language learning is supported by caring and responsive adults who talk to them, label and describe experiences and objects, and engage them in conversations.

- You can make sure that the infants, toddlers, and 2-year-olds in your care hear and practice using a lot of language. Take advantage of the many opportunities that are available every day and everywhere for supporting children's language development.

Activity

Trainer's Note: If the participants have taken part in the "Relationship-Based Turn-Taking" workshop, post the prepared chart and begin the activity by asking them to share with a partner their experiences with turn-taking after the workshop. Ask them to use the questions on the chart to guide their conversation. Then ask for two or three volunteers to share the highlights of their conversation.

Tell participants:

- This workshop will focus on using everyday experiences, routines, and environments to support young children's language development.

- You will watch the "Vocabulary and Language" segment of the *Strategies for Early Language and Literacy Development* video again. Pay attention to messages about using everyday experiences to support young children's language development.

Show the video. Then debrief with the whole group. Ask participants to share the messages they saw and heard related to everyday experiences, routines, and environments and promoting children's language development. Highlight the following points:

- Learning to listen and speak is the foundation for learning to read and write.

- Children learn by observing you. It is therefore important for you to be a good literacy role model.

- If you pay attention to children's cues, you can enhance their language and literacy learning all day during daily routines and experiences in any environment. You don't need to have or buy particular toys or games.

Ask participants to form groups of 3–4 persons and distribute Handout 3E, "Supporting Language Development Anytime, Anywhere."

Tell participants:

- Now, you'll have a chance to think about the many opportunities that are available every day and everywhere for supporting children's language development. You'll start by completing the handout in your groups.

Review the handout and point out that in each section (Indoor Experience, Routine, Outdoor Experience) there is one topic that has already been selected and one topic that they will choose as a group. Explain that for Outdoor, they should choose a familiar environment where they would take the children such as a park, a grocery store or farmer's market, a subway or train station, a pond or lake, or the neighborhood.

Allow enough time for each group to complete the handout.

Trainer's Note: If needed or if time allows, pick one experience or routine and do the activity as a whole group before having participants work in small groups.

Invite each group to share one experience, routine, or outdoor environment with the whole group. As participants share their responses, highlight the following points:

- Every experience, routine, and environment has language development opportunities!

- Be intentional. Use these opportunities to talk to children about what they see, hear, feel, taste, smell, and do.

- Have conversations with children and remember turn-taking techniques.

- Point out letters and print. Explain how the print helps communicate information.

- Remember that you are a language and literacy role model for children.

Taking The Training Home

End the workshop by inviting participants to take the training home. Suggest that they try the following:

- Review your completed Handout 3E, "Supporting Language Development Anytime, Anywhere." Try the experience, routine, and outdoor strategies your group developed with one child in your group. Use the strategies daily for 1–2 weeks. Observe how the child responds. Then try the strategies with other children in your group. Keep observing!

- Expand and practice. Remember that there are more than two experiences, routines, and outdoor environments where you can intentionally support children's language development. Work with your co-teacher or another early childhood professional in your program to develop additional strategies for those experiences, routines, and outdoor environments.

Summary

If you have conducted the three "Vocabulary and Language" workshops consecutively with these participants, summarize by making the following points:

- One of children's greatest achievements in the first 3 years of life is the development of oral language. This includes the ability to understand the words they hear and to put their own ideas and feelings into words so that they can communicate with others.

- People once thought that it wasn't important to talk to babies because they did not understand what was being said to them. We now know that adults should use every opportunity—starting at birth—to talk to babies, describe things, reassure them, and sing to them.

- Infants, toddlers, and twos need you to offer intentional experiences every day in order for them to acquire the building blocks of language and literacy.

Adapting the Workshop for Families

If you are presenting this workshop to families, consider the following adaptations:

- Create a chart with the following questions:

   What did you notice about your child when you took turns as you played?

   What was the experience like for you as the parent?

   What did you like about using the techniques? What was challenging?

- For the small-group activity after viewing the video segment, distribute Handout F3E, "Supporting Language Development Anytime, Anywhere."

- In "Taking the Training Home," suggest the following:

   Review your completed handout, "Supporting Language Development Anytime, Anywhere." Pick one of the experience, routines, or outdoor environment strategies that your group developed and try it with your child.

   Expand and practice. Remember that there are many experiences, routines, and outdoor environments through which you can support your child's language development. If you would like suggestions for what to do, work with your child's teachers to develop additional strategies.

- If participants have taken part in the three "Vocabulary and Language" workshops consecutively, include this point as you summarize:

   You can support your child's language and literacy skills during daily routines and experiences and in any environment. Pay attention to what you say and do with your child during those times. Remember, you don't need to have or buy special toys or games to help your child learn important language skills.

Notes:

Handout 3E.
Supporting Language Development Anytime, Anywhere

Indoor Experience	What a Child Might Do During This Experience	What I Can Do to Support Language Development During This Experience
Imitating and Pretending		

Routine	What a Child Might Do During This Routine	What I Can Do to Support Language Development During This Routine
Getting Dressed		

Outdoor Experience	What a Child Might Do During This Experience	What I Can Do to Support Language Development During This Experience
Outdoor Play		

Handout F3E.
Supporting Language Development Anytime, Anywhere

Indoor Experience	What My Child Might Do During This Experience	What I Can Do to Support Language Development During This Experience
Playing With Toys		

Routine	What My Child Might Do During This Routine	What I Can Do to Support Language Development During This Routine
Getting Dressed		

Outdoor Experience	What My Child Might Do During This Experience	What I Can Do to Support Language Development During This Experience
Outdoor Play		

The Sounds and Rhythms of Language

Workshops for Staff Members

WORKSHOP	KEY POINTS	MATERIALS	TIME (minutes)
The Sounds Around Us (p. 68)	Infants, toddlers, and twos develop *sound awareness*, the ability to notice and recognize different sounds. It is the first step in developing *phonological awareness,* which is the ability to hear the small units of sound in spoken language. Young children begin to develop this awareness through everyday experiences.	☐ Tape ☐ Prepared charts ☐ Sound bags ☐ DVD player and monitor, or computer and LCD projector ☐ *Strategies for Early Language and Literacy Development* video ☐ Handout 4A. The Sounds of Language ☐ Handout 4B. Sounds on a Walk	90
The Sounds of Songs (p. 78)	Music can support the development of *sound awareness*. Playing and singing songs, reciting nursery rhymes and chants, and doing fingerplays help children become aware of the sounds and rhythms of their language.	☐ Chart paper ☐ Markers ☐ Tape ☐ Prepared charts ☐ DVD player and monitor, or computer and LCD projector ☐ *Strategies for Early Language and Literacy Development* video ☐ Book of favorites (optional) ☐ Handout 4C. Exploring Language and Literacy Through Songs, Chants, Rhymes, and Fingerplays	60

WORKSHOP	KEY POINTS	MATERIALS	TIME (minutes)
Making Musical Instruments (p. 84)	Introducing rhythms to children supports their emerging language and literacy skills. As children develop language, they begin to recognize its rhythms.	☐ Chart paper ☐ Markers ☐ Materials to make musical instruments ☐ Book of favorites (optional)	90

WORKSHOP

The Sounds Around Us

☐ Tape
☐ Prepared charts
☐ Sound bags
☐ DVD player and monitor, or computer and LCD projector
☐ *Strategies for Early Language and Literacy Development* video
☐ Handout 4A
☐ Handout 4B

Preparation

Make sound bags by filling small paper bags with toys or other appropriate materials for infants, toddlers, and twos that make sounds. Prepare 3–4 sound bags per table of participants.

Prepare a chart with the following sound walk questions:

- What did you hear?
- How do you know what it was?
- What did it sound like?
- What words or phonemes (sounds that form words) might include those sounds?
- What words did you use to describe the sound?

Prepare a chart with the following sound bag questions:

- What is the item? Why do you think it is that item?
- How many are in the bag? How do you know?
- What size is the item? Does size make a difference?
- Does it sound like anything else?
- Can you imitate the sound? Describe the sound.

Preview the "Sounds in the Environment" segment of the *Strategies for Early Language and Literacy Development* video.

Duplicate the two handouts.

Optional:

Review the following material in *The Creative Curriculum® for Infants, Toddlers & Twos:*

- "The Sounds and Rhythms of Language," pages 113–114

Introduction

Introduce the workshop by reviewing Handout 4A, "The Sounds of Language."
Tell participants:

- As children's language and literacy skills emerge, they are able to distinguish sounds first in the environment and then in words.

- The ability to hear and distinguish the sounds and rhythms of language is a necessary skill for reading.

- During the first 3 years of life, the brain is very receptive to learning the sounds that make up language.

- During the preschool years, children are developing *phonological awareness*, which is the ability to hear the small units of sound in spoken language.

- During the preschool years, children

    notice rhyming words in songs, poems, fingerplays, and stories.

    enjoy playing with words, such as saying "banana-fana-fo-fana."

    begin to hear and clap the syllables in their names.

    begin to notice that some words start with the same sound.

Activity

Prepare participants for viewing the "Sounds in the Environment" segment of the *Strategies for Early Language and Literacy Development* video. Tell them:

- Close your eyes for a moment and think about all the sounds you heard today. Maybe you heard a bird singing, cars starting, the voices of family members, or coins dropping on a counter when you bought a cup of coffee.

Ask participants to list all of the sounds they heard today. Then invite several volunteers to share their lists.

Tell participants:

- Let's watch a short videoclip. We will see adults pointing out sounds to children. As you watch, list all of the sounds the children hear.

Show the video. When it is over, invite someone to share his or her list with the group.

Tell participants:

- You're now going to go on a "sound walk" to discover the kinds of sounds that are around us. Bring Handout 4B, "Sounds on a Walk," with you so that you can list all of the sounds you hear. Try not to talk during the walk so that you can hear the sounds around you.

Trainer's Note: As you plan the sound walk, consider the location and the time of year. An outside walk around the community is the best option, but, if that is not possible, plan a walk through the building. The goal of the walk is for participants to listen for various sounds and to identify what is making the sound. That can be done almost anywhere.

After the sound walk, post the sound walk questions and tell participants:

- Using these questions as a guide, share with the others at your table what you heard on the walk. Be as specific as possible when you identify a sound.

After the groups have had time to complete this activity, introduce the sound bag activity. Tell participants:

- We saw adults in the video helping children notice the sounds of toys and materials. Now we are going to explore the sounds that toys and materials make.

Post the sound bag questions. Give the following instructions:

- There are several sound bags at your table. Each bag has one or more items that make a sound when you shake the bag. Explore the sounds you hear.

- Use these questions to guide your conversation about the items and sounds.

Allow time for participants to explore the bags on their tables. Then tell them:

- This activity was designed for adults. How would you adapt it to offer an experience for infants, toddlers, and twos?

Possible responses:

> *Show the children how to make the sound.*
>
> *Repeat the name of the toy or material while the child is using it.*
>
> *Take turns with the child as we both play with the toy.*

Tell participants:

- Young children learn through hands-on explorations. They will probably want to take the toys and materials out of the bags and put them in their mouths or turn the experience into a dump-and-fill activity. Make sure the toys and materials you use are safe and age-appropriate.

End the activity by making the following points:

- Children develop sound awareness by exploring their indoor and outdoor environments.

- It is important for young children to distinguish environmental sounds as well as to make sounds. Later on, children will learn to distinguish the sounds of letters and words.

Taking The Training Home

Invite participants to take the training home. Suggest that they try the following:

- Try the sound bag activity with the children in your group. Adapt it to fit their skills and interests.

- Call attention to sounds children hear during the day: "Yes, that's an airplane," or "Oops. You dropped your spoon. What a loud noise it made!"

- Make the sounds of animals and objects: "Meow, meow" or "Vroom, vroom."

- Imitate the sounds children make and encourage them to imitate part of what you say: "I hear you saying, 'Ma-ma-ma-ma.' Now say it to me again."

- Use descriptive language to talk about the sounds children hear: "The wind sounds like it's whispering to us." "The water makes a plopping sound when it drips from the faucet."

Adapting the Workshop for Families

If you are presenting this workshop to families, consider the following adaptations:

- Use Handout F4A, "The Sounds of Language" to introduce the workshop.

- Distribute and review Handout F4B, "Sounds on a Walk" before going on the sound walk.

Notes:

Handout 4A.
The Sounds of Language

- *Phonological awareness* is the ability to hear the small units of sound in spoken language.

- Children begin to develop *phonological awareness* during the preschool years.

- Infants, toddlers, and twos develop *sound awareness*, the ability to notice and recognize different sounds. This is the first step in developing *phonological awareness*.

- Every language has its own set of sounds that are used to form words. These sounds are called *phonemes*. Children are born ready to learn these sounds.

- By 6 months of age, most children are able to babble and repeat the sounds (*phonemes*) that make up the languages they hear.

- Infants, toddlers, and twos begin to develop *sound awareness* through everyday experiences.

Handout 4B.
Sounds on a Walk

What do you hear?

What sounds are you surprised to hear?

Do you hear any sounds that you have never heard before? What are they?

Handout F4A.
The Sounds of Language

- *Phonological awareness* is the ability to hear the small units of sound in spoken language.

- Children begin to develop *phonological awareness* during the preschool years.

- Infants, toddlers, and twos develop *sound awareness*, the ability to notice and recognize different sounds. This is the first step in developing *phonological awareness*.

- Every language has its own set of sounds that are used to form words. These sounds are called *phonemes*. Children are born ready to learn these sounds.

- By 6 months of age, most children are able to babble and repeat the sounds (*phonemes*) that make up the languages they hear.

- Infants, toddlers and twos begin to develop *sound awareness* through everyday experiences.

Handout F4B.
Sounds on a Walk

What do you hear?

What sounds are you surprised to hear?

Do you hear any sounds that you have never heard before? What are they?

The Sounds of Songs

Handout 4C.
Exploring Language and Literacy
Through Songs, Chants, Rhymes, and Fingerplays

1. Name of song, chant, rhyme, or fingerplay: _____

What language and literacy skills do children learn from this song, chant, rhyme, or fingerplay?

What other skills or information might children learn?

2. Name of song, chant, rhyme, or fingerplay: _____

What language and literacy skills do children learn from this song, chant, rhyme, or fingerplay?

What other skills or information might children learn?

☐ Chart paper
☐ Markers
☐ Tape
☐ Prepared chart
☐ DVD player and monitor, or computer and LCD projector
☐ *Strategies for Early Language and Literacy Development* video
☐ Book of favorites (optional)
☐ Handout 4C

Preparation

Prepare a chart with the following prompts:

- Remember when you were young.

  What was one of your favorite childhood songs?

  What made it special?

  Who taught it to you?

  What do you remember most about the experience of listening to or singing it?

- What was it like for you to share a personal music experience?

Ask participants in advance to bring the words to a favorite rhyme, song, chant, or fingerplay that they use with the children in their group.

Duplicate the handout.

Preview the "Sounds: Rhyme, Rhythm, and Song" segment of the *Strategies for Early Language and Literacy Development* video.

Optional:

Review the following material in *The Creative Curriculum® for Infants, Toddlers & Twos:*

- "The Sounds and Rhythms of Language," pages 113–114

- "What You Can Do and Say," page 120

- "Supporting Development and Learning," page 344

- "Caring and Teaching," pages 347–351

Introduction

Introduce the workshop by telling participants:

- Music is one of the best ways to introduce children to the sounds and rhythms of language. Music can support the development of sound awareness.

- When you play and sing songs, recite nursery rhymes and chants, and do fingerplays, you are helping children become aware of the sounds and rhythms of their language.

Activity

Display the prepared questions. Ask participants to discuss them in pairs. Invite a few participants to share their thoughts with the group. Emphasize the following points:

- Often the early experiences we remember were with persons who were important to us and with whom we had positive relationships.

- For infants, toddlers, and twos, language develops through trusting relationships.

Ask:

- What are some things that these songs have in common?

Chart responses.

> ***Possible responses:***
> *Words*
> *Sounds*
> *Repetition*
> *Rhyming*
> *Predictability*
> *Pitch*
> *Movement*
> *Time when they are sung*
> *Family history*
> *Positive memories*

Ask:

- Which of those things support children's emerging language and literacy skills?

Circle the answers. If you have circled everything or almost everything on the list, point out how many literacy skills children can explore by singing songs.

Prepare participants for viewing "Sounds: Rhyme, Rhythm, and Song" in the *Strategies for Early Language and Literacy Development* video by asking them to think about the messages conveyed in that segment.

Show the video. When it is over, ask volunteers to comment. Tie their comments to the discussion about their favorite childhood songs and how music and songs support children's language and literacy development.

Distribute Handout 4C, "Exploring Language and Literacy Through Songs, Chants, Rhymes, and Fingerplays."

Instruct participants:

- Work in pairs. Share with each other the song, chant, rhyme, or fingerplay you brought to the training. Then complete the handout for each song.

Allow time for participants to complete the activity. Ask for volunteers to share one of their songs, chants, rhymes, or fingerplays and what children learn from it. As participants share, emphasize the following points:

- Young children enjoy songs, chants, rhymes, and fingerplays. Try to use them daily.

- You can use music and movement intentionally to promote children's listening skills, introduce new words, and draw attention to the sounds and structure of language. For example:

    You can recite nursery rhymes and chants and clap the beat.

    With toddlers and 2-year-olds, you can emphasize words that rhyme and words that start with the same sound when you sing, recite nursery rhymes and chants, and do fingerplays.

Trainer's Note: You can collect all of the songs, chants, rhymes, and fingerplays and bind them as a book of favorites to give to each participant or program at the end of the workshop series.

Taking The Training Home

End the workshop by inviting participants to take the training home. Suggest that they try the following:

- Sing silly songs, make up words, play with sounds, and imitate the sounds children make.

- Sing songs that encourage children to listen for and anticipate an action: "Ring around the rosie...Ashes, ashes, we all fall down!" "Open, shut them... but do not let them in!"

- Invite children to repeat the refrain from a song they have heard many times, such as "E-I-E-I-O" and fill in the rhyming word in a predictable refrain when you pause before saying the word: "With a knick-knack paddywhack, give a dog a bone, this old man came rolling ...."

- Find board books with words to familiar songs, chants, rhymes, and fingerplays. Read and sing them with your children.

- Learn lullabies that families sing so that you can sing them to the children.

- Share recording equipment with families so that they can record songs for you to play while their children are in your care.

Adapting the Workshop for Families

If you are presenting this workshop to families, consider the following adaptations:

- Distribute and review Handout F4C, "Exploring Language and Literacy Through Sounds, Chants, Rhymes, and Fingerplays" before the participants work in pairs.

- Collect all of the songs, chants, rhymes, and fingerplays and bind them as a book of favorites to give to each family at the end of the workshop series.

- Suggest that families share the rhymes, chants, songs, and lullabies they sing to their children with their children's teachers so that the teachers can sing them to the children, too.

Handout 4C.
Exploring Language and Literacy Through Songs, Chants, Rhymes, and Fingerplays

1. Name of song, chant, rhyme, or fingerplay: _____

What language and literacy skills do children learn from this song, chant, rhyme, or fingerplay?

What other skills or information might children learn?

2. Name of song, chant, rhyme, or fingerplay: _____

What language and literacy skills do children learn from this song, chant, rhyme, or fingerplay?

What other skills or information might children learn?

Handout F4C.
Exploring Language and Literacy Through Songs, Chants, Rhymes, and Fingerplays

1. Name of song, chant, rhyme, or fingerplay: _____

Can you think of language and literacy skills that your child learns from this song, chant, rhyme, or fingerplay?

What other skills or information might your child learn?

2. Name of song, chant, rhyme, or fingerplay: _____

Can you think of language and literacy skills that your child learns from this song, chant, rhyme, or fingerplay?

What other skills or information might your child learn?

Making Musical Instruments

- ☐ Chart paper
- ☐ Markers
- ☐ Tape or glue
- ☐ Art materials
- ☐ Bin of recycled materials such as toilet paper rolls, paper towel rolls, wrapping paper rolls, egg cartons, oatmeal boxes, coffee cans, and metal pie tins
- ☐ Bags of beans and rice
- ☐ Beads or buttons
- ☐ Book of favorites (optional)

Preparation

Gather materials that can be used to make musical instruments and put them on a table in the training room.

Optional:

Review the following material in *The Creative Curriculum® for Infants, Toddlers & Twos:*

- "Connecting With Music and Movement," pages 343–355

Introduction

Introduce the workshop by telling participants:

- Introducing various rhythms to children supports their emerging language and literacy skills.

- As children develop language, they begin to recognize its rhythms.

Ask:

- What are some ways we introduce children to the rhythms of language? Other rhythms?

Invite participants to share their ideas.

> *Possible responses:*
>
> *Reading stories out loud*
>
> *Talking*
>
> *Singing*
>
> *Reciting poems*
>
> *Telling stories*
>
> *Chanting*
>
> *Clapping to music*
>
> *Dancing*
>
> *Pointing out rhythmic environmental sounds, such as car alarms, trains, church bells, and ticking clocks*

Tell participants:

- In this workshop, you are going to create musical instruments and think about how you can use them to help children explore rhythm.

Activity

Invite participants to examine the materials on the table and take what they need to create a musical instrument they could use with the children in their group.

Encourage participants to share ideas and discuss what they are making. As people begin to finish their instruments, invite them to explain what they used to make the instrument and ask them to use it to perform their favorite song, chant, or rhyme. Ask how they will use these instruments with their children.

> *Possible responses:*
>
> *Make simple sound patterns*
>
> *Keep the beat of a chant or song*
>
> *Soothe infants*
>
> *Take turns using the instrument*
>
> *Imitate sounds or movement*
>
> *Explore body movements*

Tell participants:

- We know that infants, toddlers, and twos like to put things in their mouths! Remember that the materials for shaking instruments, such as beans, rice, small beads, and buttons, are choking hazards. So, making shakers is not an appropriate activity for children under 3 years of age.

Taking The Training Home

Invite participants to take the training home. Suggest that they try the following:

- Use your instrument with the children in your group. Make more instruments if you like, so that more than one child can have one.

- Invite families to help you make simple instruments such as drums, shakers, and sand blocks.

- Encourage children to explore the sounds they can make with materials such as pots and pans, wooden spoons, boxes, toilet paper rolls, and cans with safe rims.

Summary

If the participants have taken part in all three "Sounds and Rhythms of Language" workshops consecutively, summarize by making the following points:

- *Sound awareness* is the ability to notice and recognize sounds. It is the first step in developing phonological awareness.

- *Phonological awareness* is the ability to hear the small units of sound in spoken language.

- Everyday experiences help children develop sound awareness. Call children's attention to interesting sounds.

- When you talk with children, play and sing songs, recite nursery rhymes and chants, and do fingerplays, you help them become aware of the sounds and rhythms of their language.

- To help infants, toddlers, and twos acquire the building blocks of language and literacy, take the time every day for activities that help them become aware of the sounds and rhythms of their language.

Adapting the Workshop for Families

If you are presenting this workshop to families, consider the following adaptation:

- Suggest the following in addition to exploring sounds with materials found at home:

    Use the instrument with your child.

    Make other simple instruments for your child to use.

Notes:

Exploring Writing

Workshops for Staff Members

WORKSHOP	KEY POINTS	MATERIALS	TIME (minutes)
Learning About Symbols (p. 90)	Learning about symbols is an important part of getting ready to read. It helps children understand later on that a letter is associated with a sound and the word *chair*, for example, refers to what they sit on. When symbols are a part of everyday interactions and routines, children begin to understand that they have meaning.	☐ Chart paper ☐ Markers ☐ Tape ☐ Materials to create a classroom toy, game, or other activity ☐ Prepared chart ☐ Handout 5A. Strategies to Help Infants, Toddlers, and Twos Learn About Symbols and What They Mean ☐ Handout 5B. Symbols in the Community	90
Viewing the Video: "Exploring Writing" (p. 102)	Children learn about writing when they see print, hear it read aloud, and see adults writing for different reasons. Older infants, toddlers, and twos begin to experiment with writing if they are given drawing, painting, and writing tools and plenty of time to use these materials. Programs for young children can help them develop skills they will use as they learn to write.	☐ Collection of manipulatives, sensory materials, and drawing and writing materials ☐ VCR or DVD player and monitor, or computer and LCD projector ☐ *Strategies for Early Language and Literacy Development* video ☐ Handout 5C. Experiences With Print and Writing	60

WORKSHOP	KEY POINTS	MATERIALS	TIME (minutes)
Stages of Writing Development (p. 110)	Learning to write is a complex skill that takes time and practice to learn. Writing involves fine motor skills, eye-hand coordination, visual perception, understanding print concepts, and, eventually, knowledge of the alphabet. Children go through stages as they develop drawing and writing skills.	☐ Handout 5D. Stages of Writing Development ☐ Handout 5E. Children's Scribbles and Drawings ☐ Handout 5F. Children's Scribbles and Drawings: Answer Key	60

Learning About Symbols

- ☐ Chart paper
- ☐ Markers
- ☐ Tape
- ☐ Materials to create a classroom toy, game, or other activity
- ☐ Prepared chart
- ☐ Handout 5A
- ☐ Handout 5B

Preparation

Prepare a chart with the following text:

- Learning about symbols and how they communicate meaning helps young children get ready to read.

- A symbol is something that is used to represent something else.

For each table of participants, gather the following materials for creating a classroom toy, game, or other activity to introduce symbols to infants, toddlers, and twos: copies of Handout 5B, "Symbols in the Community"; magazines; newspapers; advertisements; local community papers; glue sticks or transparent tape; scissors; construction paper or card stock; yarn; hole punches.

You can also ask participants in advance to bring magazines, newspapers, advertisements, and local community papers to the workshop.

Duplicate Handout 5B, "Symbols in the Community."

Optional:

Duplicate Handout 5A, "Strategies to Help Infants, Toddlers, and Twos Learn About Symbols and What They Mean."

Optional:

Review the following material in the *The Creative Curriculum® for Infants, Toddlers & Twos*:

- Exploring Writing," pages 117–118, 121

- Chapter 12, "Imitating and Pretending," pages 309–321

- Chapter 15, "Creating With Art," pages 357–373

Introduction

Introduce the workshop by making the following points:

- Young children learn that symbols communicate meaning. For example, a child learns that a picture looks like his mother, but it is not really his mother. He learns that a pretend phone is not a real phone and that a doll is not a real baby.

- When graphic symbols, such as pictures, photographs, words, signs, and logos are part of everyday interactions and routines, children begin to understand that they have meaning.

- Learning about symbols is an important part of getting ready to read. This helps children understand later on that a letter is associated with a sound and that the word *chair,* for example, refers to what they sit on.

Activity

Post the prepared chart paper. Tell participants:

- In this activity, you will explore symbols and how children learn about them through daily interactions and activities.

Give each table a piece of chart paper and ask that it be folded in half and labeled "Symbols in Infant, Toddler, and Twos Rooms" in the left-hand column, and "Symbols in the Community" in the right-hand column.

Give the following directions:

- Working together at your table, think of examples of symbols in each category and list them on the chart paper.

Allow time for the groups to complete the activity. Then, debrief by asking each group to share its responses.

Possible responses for "Symbols in Infant, Toddler, and Twos Rooms":

Photos of children and families

Children's artwork

Dramatic play materials

Dolls, stuffed animals, and puppets

Toy vehicles

Books

Children's names on cubbies

Labels on shelves and containers

Daily schedules

Calendars

Exit sign

Possible responses for "Symbols in the Community":

Restaurant and store logos

Stop sign

Books, magazines, and newspapers

Menus, especially those with pictures of food

Store signs

As participants share, point out the following:

- Symbols are used to communicate information.

- Children often use everyday objects as symbols, such as when a 2-year-old uses a block as a phone.

- When young children begin to understand that one thing can stand for another, they are on their way to learning that alphabet letters stand for letter sounds and that written words stand for spoken language.

Lead a discussion and record participants' responses on chart paper.

Possible responses:

> *Provide a variety of print and picture materials*
>
> *Talk about and point out pictures, signs, words, logos*
>
> *Comment positively on children's attempts to draw or write*
>
> *Display children's drawings and scribbles*
>
> *Let children see us writing notes and lists, and explain what we're writing and why.*

As participants share their responses, include the following points in the discussion:

- When we are intentional about helping infants and toddlers learn about symbols, they

  > show interest in pictures and photos

  > recognize and interpret pictures (for example, point to an adult female in a family photo and say, "mama"; or know where their cubbies are and point to their pictures or names on the cubbies)

  > recognize and name logos for familiar foods, such as Cheerios®

  > develop more control of finger and hand movements

  > learn how to hold and use utensils and writing tools

  > show that they understand that marks on paper represent something (for example, point to shapes and squiggles on paper and say, "Doggie" or ask you to write his name on a picture)

Trainer's Note: This activity can be done in groups of 3–4 participants or by table, as well as with the entire group. For small groups or tables, ask participants to write their ideas on Handout 5A, "Strategies to Help Infants, Toddlers, and Twos Learn About Symbols and What They Mean." Then invite participants to share their responses by group or table.

Tell participants:

- You will now have an opportunity to create a classroom material, game, or other activity to introduce symbols to infants, toddlers, and twos and help them begin to learn what the symbols mean.

- Break into small groups and form tables according to the age of the children with whom you work: infants, toddlers, or twos.

Give each group a collection of materials and copies of Handout 5B. Invite them to create a game, activity, or material to use with the children in their room. Allow enough time for participants to complete the activity. When they are done, ask for volunteers to share their creations and how they would use them to introduce symbols to children.

End the activity by reinforcing the following points:

- When graphic symbols, such as pictures, photographs, words, signs, and logos are part of everyday interactions and routines, children begin to understand that they have meaning.

- When young children begin to understand that one thing can stand for another thing, they are on their way to learning that alphabet letters stand for letter sounds and that written words stand for spoken language.

- Children need to learn that print is meaningful and that they can learn how to write It takes children several years to figure out these concepts.

Taking The Training Home

End the workshop by inviting participants to take the training home. Suggest that they try the following:

- Use the game, activity, or material with the children in your room. Observe their responses. Do they have fun with it? Does it keep their interest? Remember to talk about what the children see, hear, and do as they engage in the game or activity.

- Act intentionally! Think about the strategies that we talked about in this workshop for helping infants, toddlers, and twos learn about symbols and what they mean. Pick one that you haven't tried yet or want to use more often. Incorporate it into your daily routines and experiences.

Adapting the Workshop for Families

If you are presenting this workshop to families, consider the following adaptations:

- Duplicate Handout F5B, "Symbols in the Community" for use in creating the game, activity, or material.

- For the table activity using chart paper, ask participants to label the left column "Symbols in My Home" and the right column, "Symbols in My Community."

- Duplicate Handout F5A, "Strategies to Help Your Child Learn About Symbols and What They Mean" if you do the activity in small groups or tables.

Notes:

Handout 5A.
Strategies to Help Infants, Toddlers, and Twos Learn About Symbols and What They Mean

Infants

Toddlers

Twos

Handout 5B.
Symbols in the Community

Public Library

Playground

 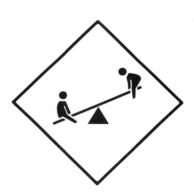

Bus Stop

Airport

Phone

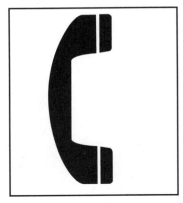 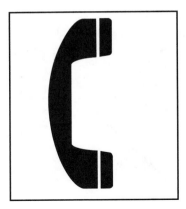

Stop Sign

Handout F5A.
Strategies to Help Your Child Learn About Symbols and What They Mean

Infants

Toddlers

Twos

Handout F5B.
Symbols in the Community

Public Library

Playground

Bus Stop

Airport

Phone

 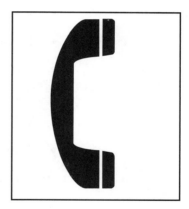

Stop sign

WORKSHOP

Viewing the Video: "Exploring Writing"

Handout 5C.
Experiences With Print and Writing

I already provide these experiences with print and writing:

1. _____
2. _____
3. _____

I want to try this experience:

_____

☐ Collection of manipulatives, sensory materials, and drawing and writing materials

☐ VCR or DVD player and monitor, or computer and LCD projector

☐ *Strategies for Early Language and Literacy Development* video

☐ Handout 5C

Preparation

Gather the following toys and materials:

- Knobbed puzzles
- Playdough
- Chalk and chalkboard
- Collage materials
- Markers and paper bags
- Magazines and scissors
- Two to 3 colors of finger paint
- Finger paints and paper
- Sand in a box
- Large beads with yarn or string
- Shape sorters
- Stacking rings or stacking cups
- White paper and crayons
- Construction paper

Set up 3–4 different stations around the room with the following materials:

- *Manipulatives*, such as knobbed puzzles, beads and yarn, shape sorters, stacking rings or stacking cups, simple matching or memory games
- *Sensory materials*, such as playdough, sand in a box, finger paint and paper, collage materials
- *Drawing and writing* materials, such as chalk and chalkboard, markers, paper bags, white paper, crayons, construction paper, magazines, scissors

Preview "Exploring Writing" in the *Strategies for Early Language and Literacy Development* video.

Duplicate the handout.

Optional:

Review the following material in *The Creative Curriculum® for Infants, Toddlers & Twos:*

- "Exploring Writing," pages 117–118, 121

- Chapter 11, "Playing With Toys," pages 291–307

- Chapter 15, "Creating With Art," pages 357–373

Introduction

Introduce the workshop by making the following points:

Reading and writing go together. Children learn about writing when they see print, hear it read aloud, and see you writing for different reasons.

Older infants, toddlers, and twos can begin to learn about and experiment with writing if you give them drawing, painting, and writing tools and plenty of time to use them.

Activity

Trainer's Note: If the participants have taken part in the "Learning About Symbols" workshop, begin the activity by asking them to talk about how children responded to the symbol game, activity, or material. Also, ask what strategies they tried after the workshop to help children learn about symbols.

Prepare participants for viewing "Exploring Writing" in the *Strategies for Early Language and Literacy Development* video.

Tell them:

- In the "Exploring Writing" video segment that you are about to watch, you will see examples of symbols and examples of ways to offer children reading and writing experiences.

- As you watch the video, pay attention to the experiences you see. Make a note of at least three experiences that you already provide for children and one experience that you haven't tried yet. Write them on your Handout 5C, "Experiences With Print and Writing," as you notice them.

Distribute the handout and show the video. Then, invite volunteers to share one experience they already provide and one experience they want to try.

Tell participants:

- You will now have a chance to play with some toys and materials. Several stations of toys and materials are set up around the room. For the next 10–15 minutes, find and play with one or two toys or materials. Explore the toys or materials and experiment with different ways to use them.

- When you are done, go back to your table and record which toys or materials you played with and how you used them.

Allow time for the activity and then debrief with the whole group. Ask for volunteers to talk about what they played with. After they have shared, invite participants to play with the same toys or materials they used the first time. Explain that this time they will focus on how the toys and materials can support the development of writing skills. Give participants another 10–15 minutes for this activity.

Debrief with the whole group. Ask for volunteers to share what they played with and how the toy or material can be used to support young children's development of writing skills.

Possible responses:

Strengthen hand muscles

Practice eye-hand coordination

Learn how to grasp and hold writing tools

Practice using different writing tools

Enjoy making marks on paper or other surfaces

Strengthen memory skills (later, children will need to remember what each alphabet letter looks like and how to make each one)

As participants share, point out the following:

- You can help children develop important skills to support their progress in learning to write. These include the following:

    Fine motor skills—using and controlling the small muscles that are used to pick up, hold, and control tools for drawing and writing

    Attention skills—focusing on something for a period of time

    Memory—remembering sounds, words, and, eventually, letters

    Language—learning new vocabulary and language structure

Taking The Training Home

End the workshop by inviting participants to take the training home. Suggest that they try the following:

- Review your "Experiences With Print and Writing" handout. How often do you offer the experiences that you already provide? Are there experiences that you can provide more regularly or daily? Plan and carry out the experience that you haven't tried yet.

- Act intentionally. Look for opportunities during daily routines and experiences to help children develop the fine motor, attention, memory, and language skills that support their learning to write.

Adapting the Workshop for Families

If you are presenting this workshop to families, consider the following adaptations:

- As you prepare participants to view the "Exploring Writing" video segment, ask them to make a note of two experiences they already have with their child and one experience they haven't tried yet. Ask them to write the experiences on Handout F5C, "Experiences With Print and Writing" as they notice them in the video.

- Duplicate, distribute and review Handout F5D, "What You Can Do at Home to Support Your Child's Experiences With Symbols and Writing" and Handout F5E, "Recipes for Playdough, Baker's Clay, and Goop," in addition to providing suggestions for things to try at home.

Handout 5C.
Experiences With Print and Writing

I already provide these experiences with print and writing:

1. _____

2. _____

3. _____

I want to try this experience:

_____

Handout F5C.
Experiences With Print and Writing

I already provide these experiences with print and writing for my child:

1. _____

2. _____

3. _____

I want to try this experience with my child:

_____

Handout F5D.
What You Can Do at Home to Support Your Child's Experiences With Symbols and Writing

- Give your child items that she can use as props to inspire pretend play. Examples are dolls and doll blankets; telephones (toy or real); pots, pans, and plastic dishes; plastic people and animals; transportation toys, such as cars, trucks, and boats; and various ride-on toys.

- Play make-believe with your child. Encourage him to pretend with you by asking questions; offering a new prop; and taking on a pretend role, yourself.

- Go for a walk around your neighborhood with your child. Point out things such as fire hydrants; stop signs; store signs and billboards; and informational signs that have symbols, such as for the public library, bus stop, and so on.

- Show and talk about family photographs and pictures in books: "This is a picture of Mommy and Daddy." "Can you find the picture of the puppy on this page?"

- Let your child see you writing and talk about what you are doing: "I'm making a list of what I need to buy so we can make pancakes tomorrow."

- Point out print in the environment, such as letters on alphabet blocks, children's clothing, or signs in the community: "Look, that sign says 'stop.' There's a letter *T* just like in your name, Tómas."

- Provide simple writing tools such as large crayons, water-based markers, and large chalk for your toddler or 2-year-old. Offer plenty of plain paper so that she can use these tools to make marks, scribble, and explore writing.
  - Do not expect your child to draw or write something you will be able to recognize.
  - Instead, show your interest in what your child is doing by describing her actions: "You made lots of different marks on the paper. These are round circles, and these are lines."

- Give your child paper to tear. This helps build the small muscles in his hands and eye-hand coordination. These skills are important for holding writing tools. If you have glue or paste, let your child create a collage with the torn pieces of paper.

- Make simple art materials such as playdough or goop with your child. When your child squeezes, pounds, and pokes playdough or goop, she builds up the small muscles in her hands and her eye-hand coordination.

Handout F5E.
Recipes for Playdough, Baker's Clay, and Goop

Cloud Dough

6 cups flour

1 cup salad oil

Water to bind (about 1 cup)

Knead ingredients together. The final product will feel oily and very smooth. Store it in an airtight container

Basic Playdough

3 cups flour

1 cup salt

1 cup water

¼ cup salad oil

Knead all the ingredients together. Form it into balls. Store it in an airtight container.

Cooked Playdough

2 cups cornstarch

1 cup baking soda

1 cup water

Mix all the ingredients together and cook over a medium heat. Stir constantly until the mixture forms a ball. Allow it to cool slightly and knead. Store in plastic wrap in the refrigerator.

Once cooked playdough hardens, it can be painted.

Baker's Clay

4 cups flour

1 cup salt

1½ cups warm water

Mix all the ingredients together. Shape it into a ball. Store it in an airtight container.

Goop

3 cups cornstarch

2 cups warm water

Gradually add water to the corn starch. Mix the ingredients together with your hands. Goop is ready to use when it changes from being lumpy to satiny.

Goop hardens in the air and turns to liquid when it is held. It resists punching, but a light touch causes a finger to sink in.

Stages of Writing Development

☐ Handout 5D
☐ Handout 5E
☐ Handout 5F

Preparation

Duplicate Handouts 5D and 5E for participants. Handout 5F is the answer key for 5E .

Introduction

Introduce the activity by making the following points:

- Learning to write is a complex skill, and it takes time and practice to learn. Writing involves many skills, such as eye-hand coordination, visual perception, fine motor skills, understanding print concepts, and, eventually, knowledge of the alphabet.

- Children go through stages as they develop drawing and writing skills and construct understandings about writing.

- Mobile infants, toddlers, and twos are fascinated when they see you write. They want to imitate what you do. If children see you writing and hear you talk about what you are writing and why, they will begin to understand the purposes of writing.

Activity

Trainer's Note: If participants have taken part in the "Viewing the Video: Exploring Writing," workshop, begin the activity by asking them to share how they have helped children explore writing since the workshop.

Tell participants:

- This workshop focuses on stages that infants, toddlers, and twos go through while learning how to write and on supporting their beginning attempts at making marks.

- You will have a chance to look at some examples of children's writing to determine what stages of writing the samples represent.

Distribute Handout 5D, "Stages of Writing for Infants, Toddlers, and Twos," and review it with participants.

Distribute Handout 5E, "Children's Scribbles and Drawings."

Tell participants:

- You will have 10 minutes with your group to identify the developmental stage of each writing sample.

Allow time for the activity. Then invite participants to talk about their answers. Make the following points:

- Children of the same age may be at different stages of writing skill development.

- Drawing is an important part of learning to how to write.

- For some children, the desire to write comes before the desire to read.

- Direct, formal instruction in writing is not appropriate for young children. You can support children by providing writing materials and opportunities to practice using the materials, and by writing where children can see you.

- However, if children ask you the name of a letter or to show them how to write an alphabet letter or a word, don't say no! You have been presented a teachable moment, and you can use it to help children become more aware of letters and words and to model writing.

Now ask participants to imagine themselves in the following situation:

- You are teaching yourself a new skill, such as sewing, making jewelry, or carpentry. You just spent a long time figuring something out, such as using the zigzag stitch on a sewing machine, welding pieces of silver together, or building a bird feeder. You are excited about your accomplishment, and you decide to show it off to someone who is an expert in that area. The expert gives you positive feedback about your work but also sees that you've made some mistakes. What could the expert say to encourage you to keep learning this new skill?

Ask for volunteers to share their responses and lead a discussion as they do. Explain the following:

- Young children are in a similar position when they are just learning about writing. They make what adults consider to be mistakes. At these very early stages of making marks, resist the urge to correct children. A better strategy is to encourage children to continue their mark-making explorations.

Then ask participants:

- How would you offer encouragement in the following situations?:

    A toddler makes lines and circles in finger paint. Then, he covers them up and repeats the process over and over again.

    A child who is almost 3 years old makes a drawing and does some scribble writing under the picture. He asks you to read the scribble writing.

    A 2-year-old sees the first letter of her name on a sign. She points to it and says, "Look! My name!"

Lead a discussion of possible responses, and ask participants to share other examples of how they responded to a child's mark-making with encouragement rather than correction.

Taking The Training Home

End the workshop by inviting participants to take the training home. Suggest that they try the following:

- Save children's drawings and scribbles over time. Use your "Stages of Writing for Infants, Toddlers, and Twos" handout to determine children's writing stages and to see progress. Share the drawings and scribbles with children's families so that they can see the development as well.

- Look for opportunities to model writing for a purpose and ways to incorporate drawing and scribbling into children's daily routines and experiences.

Summary

If the participants have taken part in the three "Exploring Writing" workshops consecutively, summarize by making the following points:

- Remember that reading and writing go together. Children learn about writing when they see print, hear it read aloud, and see you writing for different reasons.

- By offering intentional experiences every day, you will be helping infants, toddlers, and twos acquire the building blocks for learning how to write.

- Children who have lots of language and literacy experiences are usually ready to continuing learning to read and write when they get to kindergarten and beyond.

- Children without many of these foundational experiences often are not ready to continue learning to read and write when they get to kindergarten, and they may fall behind in later school years.

Adapting the Workshop for Families

If you are presenting this workshop to families, consider the following adaptation:

- Duplicate Handouts F5F, "Stages of Writing for Infants, Toddlers, and 2-Year-Olds," F5G, "Children's Scribbles and Drawings," and F5H, "Children's Scribbles and Drawings: Answer Key."

- If participants have taken part in the three "Exploring Writing" workshops consecutively, include these points as you summarize:

    There are many things that you already do to help your child learn about symbols and writing.

    You can use everyday routines, experiences, and materials found in your home and community to help your child gain language and literacy skills.

Handout 5D.
Stages of Writing for Infants, Toddlers, and Twos

Random Scribbling: Infants may begin to make random marks on paper with a writing tool, such as a large crayon or marker, as early as 18 months. Some may start at an even younger age. Older infants and toddlers sometimes make patches of marks of one kind, then a new patch of a different kind. Toddlers may hold a writing tool in their fist and move their hand in broad strokes across the paper. They may draw horizontal and some vertical lines as well as make circular marks. At this stage, infants and toddlers enjoy the physical experience of making marks and are not concerned about what the picture looks like.

Controlled Scribbling: Older toddlers and twos are developing fine motor skills and eye-hand coordination. They can better control their mark-making, and their scribbles are less random. They may make the same lines and circle shapes over and over again. Two-year-olds begin to experiment with different marks, such as lines, dots, and zigzags, as well as with different colors and writing tools. They may make a series of looped scribbles and tell you it is a picture of their mother, or scribble all over a piece of paper and tell you it is a letter. Some older twos draw lines and make marks that look like letters (sometimes called mock letters).

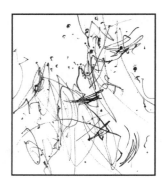

Shape Drawing and Scribble Writing: By the age of 3, most children understand that drawing and writing are different. Some children start to separate their drawings and scribbles on a page. Some children will name what the shapes in their drawing represent. Scribble writing may look like a chain of connected loops and lines or have repeated shapes.

Handout 5E.
Children's Scribbles and Drawings

A: Random Scribbling   B: Controlled Scribbling   C: Shape Drawing and Scribble Writing

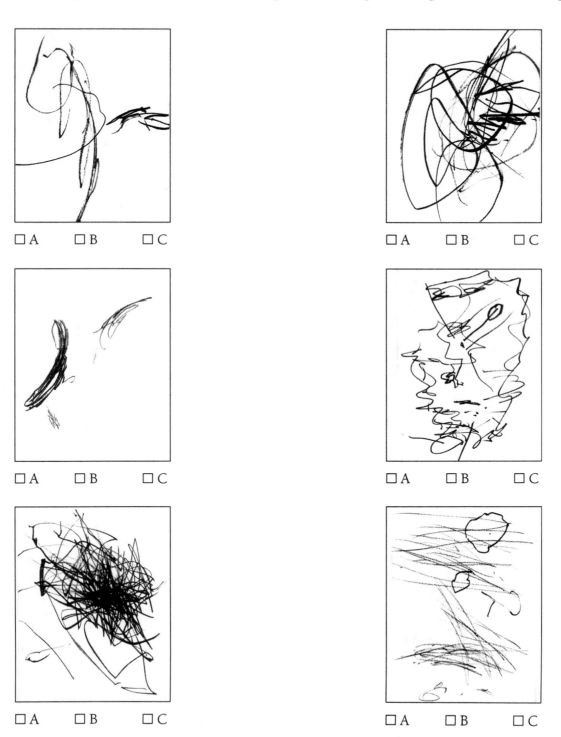

☐ A   ☐ B   ☐ C

☐ A   ☐ B   ☐ C

☐ A   ☐ B   ☐ C

☐ A   ☐ B   ☐ C

☐ A   ☐ B   ☐ C

☐ A   ☐ B   ☐ C

Handout 5F.
Children's Scribbles and Drawings: Answer Key

A: Random Scribbling   B: Controlled Scribbling   C: Shape Drawing and Scribble Writing

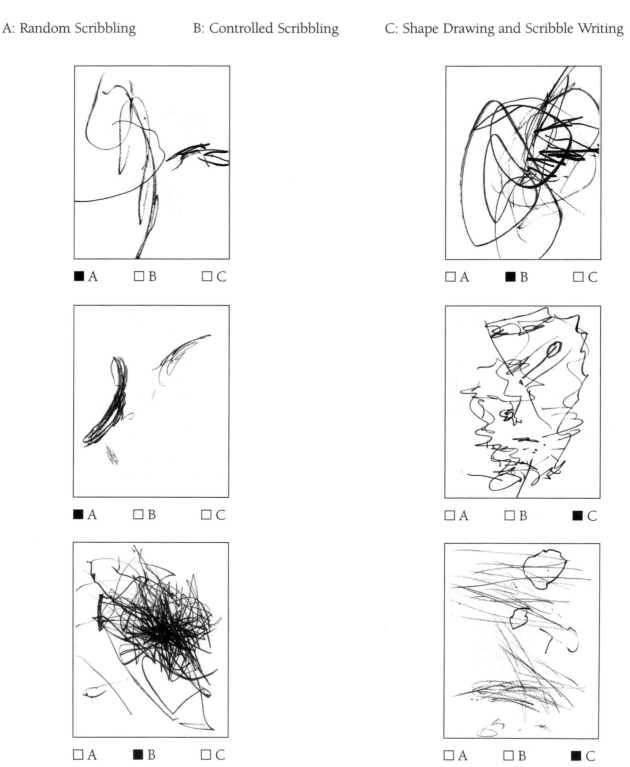

Handout F5F.
Stages of Writing for Infants, Toddlers, and 2-Year-Olds

Random Scribbling: Infants may begin to make random marks on paper with a writing tool, such as a large crayon or marker, as early as 18 months. Some may start at an even younger age. Older infants and toddlers sometimes make patches of marks of one kind, then a new patch of a different kind. Toddlers may hold a writing tool in their fist and move their hand in broad strokes across the paper. They may draw horizontal and some vertical lines as well as make circular marks. At this stage, infants and toddlers enjoy the physical experience of making marks and are not concerned about what the picture looks like.

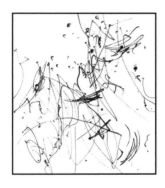

Controlled Scribbling: Older toddlers and 2-year-olds are developing fine motor skills and eye-hand coordination. They can better control their mark-making, their scribbles are less random. They may make the same lines and circle shapes over and over again. Two-year-olds begin to experiment with different marks, such as lines, dots, and zigzags, as well as with different colors and writing tools. They may make a series of looped scribbles and tell you it is a picture of you, or scribble all over a piece of paper and tell you it is a letter. Some older 2-year-olds draw lines and make marks that look like letters (sometimes called mock letters).

Shape Drawing and Scribble Writing: By the age of 3, most children understand that drawing and writing are different. Some children start to separate their drawings and scribbles on a page. Some children will name what the shapes in their drawing represent. Scribble writing may look like a chain of connected loops and lines or have repeated shapes.

Handout F5G.
Children's Scribbles and Drawings

A: Random Scribbling   B: Controlled Scribbling   C: Shape Drawing and Scribble Writing

☐ A   ☐ B   ☐ C

☐ A   ☐ B   ☐ C

☐ A   ☐ B   ☐ C

☐ A   ☐ B   ☐ C

☐ A   ☐ B   ☐ C

☐ A   ☐ B   ☐ C

Handout F5H.
Children's Scribbles and Drawings: Answer Key

A: Random Scribbling   B: Controlled Scribbling   C: Shape Drawing and Scribble Writing

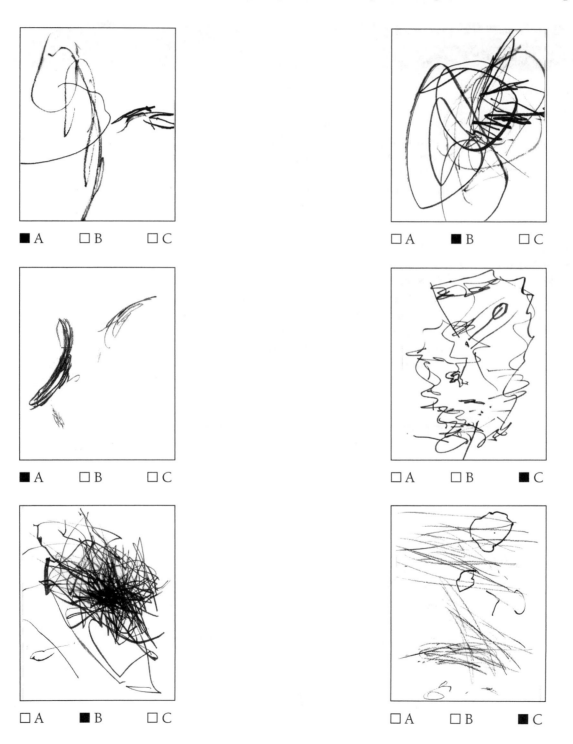

■ A   □ B   □ C   □ A   ■ B   □ C

■ A   □ B   □ C   □ A   □ B   ■ C

□ A   ■ B   □ C   □ A   □ B   ■ C

Enjoying Stories and Books

Workshops for Staff Members

WORKSHOP	KEY POINTS	MATERIALS	TIME (minutes)
Telling Stories (p. 122)	Oral storytelling is a way that cultures pass beliefs, values, and traditions from one generation to the next. It supports young children's literacy learning, knowledge, and understanding of the world, and their social-emotional well-being.	☐ Chart paper ☐ Markers ☐ Tape ☐ Handout 6A. Building a Story to Tell ☐ Handout 6B. Tips for Storytelling	60
Viewing the Video: "Enjoying Stories and Books" (p. 130)	Reading books and sharing your pleasure in language and stories are some of the most important experiences adults can offer infants, toddlers, and twos. Children develop a foundation for literacy when they regularly hear books read aloud and have opportunities to explore them firsthand.	☐ DVD player and monitor, or computer and LCD projector ☐ *Strategies for Early Language and Literacy Development* video ☐ Handout 6C. "Enjoying Stories and Books": A Viewing Guide	45

WORKSHOP	KEY POINTS	MATERIALS	TIME (minutes)
Choosing Books for Infants, Toddlers, and Twos (p. 136)	Books should be a regular part of every program for young children. High-quality books make sharing them with children even more enjoyable. Keep children's developmental abilities in mind and look for books that respect diversity and promote inclusion. With many excellent books to touch, look at, and listen to, children grow to love books.	☐ Chart paper ☐ Markers ☐ Tape ☐ A collection of books for infants, toddlers, and twos for each table ☐ Handout 6D. Good Books for Infants, Toddlers, and Twos ☐ Handout 6E. Choosing Good Books for Infants, Toddlers, and Twos ☐ Handout 6F. General Tips for Reading and Storytelling With Children ☐ Handout 6G. More Tips for Enjoying Stories and Books With Infants, Toddlers, and Twos	60
Making a Book (p. 152)	Young children, especially toddlers and twos, love to see pictures and hear stories about themselves and their families. Homemade books can provide children with a connection between home and early childhood programs.	☐ Chart paper ☐ Markers ☐ Tape ☐ Bookmaking materials ☐ DVD player and monitor, or computer and LCD projector ☐ *Strategies for Early Language and Literacy Development* video ☐ Handout 6H. Making Books for Children	90

Telling Stories

Preparation

Prepare a story to tell participants that is 5–7 minutes long. Choose an experience that was important to you, an event that happened when you were young, or a story that family members told you when you were growing up. For example, you might choose a story about how relatives came to the United States, a fable, or a story that has been passed from one generation to the next.

Prepare four charts with the following headings to hang around the training room:

- Characters' names

- Setting (where the story takes place) and action (what happens)

- Challenge to overcome or something that needs to be accomplished

- How the challenge is overcome

Duplicate the two handouts.

Optional:

Review the following material in *The Creative Curriculum® for Infants, Toddlers & Twos*:

- "Enjoying Books and Stories," pages 115–117

- "What You Can Do and Say," page 120

- Chapter 13, "Enjoying Stories and Books," pages 323–340

☐ Chart paper
☐ Markers
☐ Tape
☐ Handout 6A
☐ Handout 6B

Introduction

Introduce storytelling by explaining that children can understand the stories they hear before they can read stories, themselves. Tell participants:

- Storytelling is one of the oldest art forms.

- Most people want to express themselves, share their life stories with others, and hear others' stories.

- Even very young children want to tell stories.

- Telling stories is an important way to support young children's language and literacy learning.

- Children learn many important things while they are listening to stories: the sounds and structure of language, new words, information about themselves and their families, and much more.

ACTIVITY

Tell participants that you are going to tell them a short story. Ask them to think about what infants, toddlers, and twos learn from hearing stories and to write their ideas about stories as they listen to you.

After you have told the story, ask for volunteers to talk about what children learn from stories. Write their responses on chart paper.

Possible responses:

They learn about themselves.

They learn about their culture, language, family, and community history.

They learn how to relate to and get along with others.

They hear the sounds and rhythms of language.

They learn new words.

They learn the structure of stories.

They learn to listen as a story is told.

They learn that they can communicate their thoughts, ideas, and feelings, not only with words but with gestures and facial expressions.

During the discussion emphasize that storytelling is a way that people pass their beliefs, values, and traditions from one generation to the next. Tell them that storytelling supports young children's literacy learning, knowledge and understanding of the world, and social-emotional well-being.

Ask participants to form groups of 3–4 persons according to the ages of the children they work with: infants, toddlers, or twos. Distribute and review Handout 6A, "Building a Story to Tell." Point out the four charts throughout the room, and give each group a marker of a different color. Give the following directions:

- Talk about and list the abilities and interests of the children with whom you work. You can think of a specific child when you make your list, or you can think about children of that age-group generally.

- Pick one ability or interest on your list and develop a short story that addresses it to tell to a child or a small group of children. Use Handout 6A to help you develop the story.

- When your group is done, have someone from the group write the information about your story on each chart.

Trainer's Note: If there is time, demonstrate the activity with a sample story before the groups develop their stories.

Allow time for each group to write its story. When all the groups are done, ask for a volunteer from each group to read its story. Remind the participants that the charts will help them think about the elements of stories and how easily they can create stories to tell their children.

End the activity by distributing and reviewing Handout 6B, "Tips for Storytelling."

Taking The Training Home

Invite participants to take the training home. Suggest that they try the following:

- Create and tell a story to a child or small group of children.

- Incorporate storytelling into your daily routines and experiences with children.

- Keep track of when you tell stories, what kind of stories you tell, and how children respond to the stories.

- Share the stories you tell children with their families.

Adapting the Workshop for Families

If you are presenting this workshop to families, consider the following adaptations:

- Distribute and review Handout F6A, "Building a Story to Tell" in preparation for the small-group storytelling activity. For the first direction, tell participants:

  Talk about and list the abilities and interests of your children. For example, what new skills have you seen your child using? What are your child's favorite activities?

  Continue with the rest of the directions.

- End the activity by distributing and reviewing Handout F6B, "Tips for Storytelling."

- In "Taking the Training Home," substitute the last suggestion with the following:

  Share the stories you tell with your child's teachers.

Handout 6A.
Building a Story to Tell

What are the names of the characters?

Where does the story take place (setting)?

What happens?

What challenge does the character have to overcome? What does the character have to accomplish?

How is the challenge overcome?

Handout 6B.
Tips for Storytelling

- Make up stories with a child in your group as the main character.

- Tell stories in which the main character does what the children did that day. The main character does not have to be a child.

- Invite family members to share stories about their life experiences.

- Use familiar storytelling phrases, such as, "Once upon a time…," "They lived happily every after," "In a far-away land…," and "The end."

- Change your voice to portray different characters.

- Involve children by having them add sound effects or motions.

- Use props, such as old hats, puppets, and stuffed animals, as well as household items that can stand for something else, such as a pot for a helmet or a piece of fabric for a cape.

- Involve older toddlers and twos by encouraging them to repeat a refrain or supply a missing word.

- Take turns telling parts of a familiar story with older toddlers and twos.

- Laugh and have fun!

Handout F6A.
Building a Story to Tell

What is the name of the character?

Where does the story take place (setting)?

What happens?

What challenge does the character have to overcome? What does the character have to accomplish?

How is the challenge overcome?

Handout F6B.
Tips for Storytelling

- Make up stories with your child as the main character.

- Tell stories about when you and other family members were children.

- Tell stories about your child when she was younger.

- Tell stories where the main character does what your child did that day. The main character does not have to be a child.

- Use familiar storytelling phrases, such as, "Once upon a time…," "They lived happily every after," "In a far-away land…," and "The end."

- Change your voice to portray different characters.

- Involve your child by having him add sound effects or motions.

- Use props, such as old hats, puppets, and stuffed animals, as well as household items that can • stand for something else, such as a pot for a helmet or a piece of fabric for a cape.

- Involve your older toddler or 2-year-old by encouraging her to repeat a refrain or supply a missing word.

- Take turns telling parts of a familiar story with your older toddler or 2-year-old.

- Laugh and have fun with your child, regardless of age!

Viewing the Video: "Enjoying Stories and Books"

☐ DVD player and monitor, or computer and LCD projector

☐ *Strategies for Early Language and Literacy Development* video

☐ Handout 6C

Preparation

Preview the "Enjoying Stories and Books" segment of the *Strategies for Early Language and Literacy Development* video.

Duplicate the handout.

Optional:

Review the following material in *The Creative Curriculum® for Infants, Toddlers & Twos:*

- "Enjoying Books and Stories," pages 115–117
- "What You Can Do and Say," page 120
- Chapter 13, "Enjoying Stories and Books," pages 323–340

Introduction

Introduce the workshop by making the following points:

- Reading to children is a powerful way to contribute to their language and literacy development. Children who are read to often and from an early age usually enter school with more advanced language and better listening skills than those who have not had the same experiences.

- Sharing stories and books with young children can become a treasured time in a teacher's day.

Activity

Trainer's Note: If participants have already taken part in the "Telling Stories" workshop, begin the activity by asking them to share their experiences with telling stories to children. Ask whether and how their storytelling practices have changed since the workshop.

Ask participants to think about and write their answers to the following questions:

- Do you recall being read to as a child?
- What positive memories do you have of the experience?
- Did you have a favorite book you wanted to hear over and over?

Ask volunteers to share their memories.

Prepare participants for viewing the *Strategies for Early Language and Literacy Development* video segment "Enjoying Stories and Books." Distribute and have the participants read Handout 6C, "'Enjoying Stories and Books': A Viewing Guide." Ask participants to keep the questions in mind while watching the video.

After viewing the video, lead the group in a discussion of the handout questions.

> *Possible responses for the first question:*
> *Homemade books*
> *Board books*
> *Cloth books*
> *Paperback books*
> *Hardback books*
>
> *Possible responses for the second question:*
> *Small-group book reading*
> *One-on-one reading*
>
> *Possible responses for the third question:*
> *Show the cover of the book*
> *Say the author's name*
> *Discuss the pictures*
> *Help the child relate the book to his life*
> *Allow the child to turn pages (even if she does so out of order)*
> *Follow the child's lead*
> *Repeat favorite lines*

Use this discussion to lead into the workshop, "Choosing Books for Infants, Toddlers, and Twos," or end by making the following points:

- Reading books and sharing your pleasure in language and stories are some of the most important experiences you can offer infants, toddlers, and twos.

- Children develop a foundation for literacy when they regularly hear books read aloud and have opportunities to explore them firsthand.

- Most children who enjoy being read to develop a love for books that will last throughout their lives, enriching their experiences and stretching their imaginations.

Adapting the Workshop for Families

If you are presenting this workshop to families, consider the following adaptations:

- Distribute and review Handout F6C, "Enjoying Stories and Books: A Viewing Guide" before watching the video segment.

Notes:

Handout 6C.
"Enjoying Stories and Books": A Viewing Guide

In the video, what kinds of books do the infants, toddlers, and twos have?

What reading experiences are taking place?

How do teachers make book reading an interactive language experience?

Handout F6C.
"Enjoying Stories and Books": A Viewing Guide

In the video, what kinds of books do the infants, toddlers, and 2-year-olds have?

What reading experiences are taking place?

How do teachers make book reading an interactive language experience?

WORKSHOP

Choosing Books for Infants, Toddlers, and Twos

(The materials list continues on the next page.)

Preparation

Use Handout 6D, "Good Books for Infants, Toddlers, and Twos," to select books for infants, toddlers, and twos, and put a collection of books at every workshop table. Each collection should include board books, washable books, softcover books, and hardcover books. Include books that show children with disabilities and children of the cultures in the program and larger community. You can also ask participants in advance to bring two of their favorite books that they read to infants, toddlers, and twos.

Duplicate the four handouts. Make enough copies of Handout 6E, "Choosing Good Books for Infants, Toddlers, and Twos," so that each participant can review two or three books.

Optional:

Review the following material in *The Creative Curriculum® for Infants, Toddlers & Twos*:

- "Enjoying Books and Stories," pages 115–117

- "What You Can Do and Say," page 120

- Chapter 13, "Enjoying Stories and Books," pages 323–340

Introduction

Introduce the workshop by making the following points:

- Books must be a regular part of your program.

- All you need are books and comfortable places for children to look at them—on their own and with you—and to hear them read aloud.

- With many excellent books to touch, look at, and listen to, children grow to love books.

- Even young infants who do not yet understand the messages found in books learn from exploring them.

- Children can look at books in many places such as on the floor, on their cots, and in a shady area outdoors.

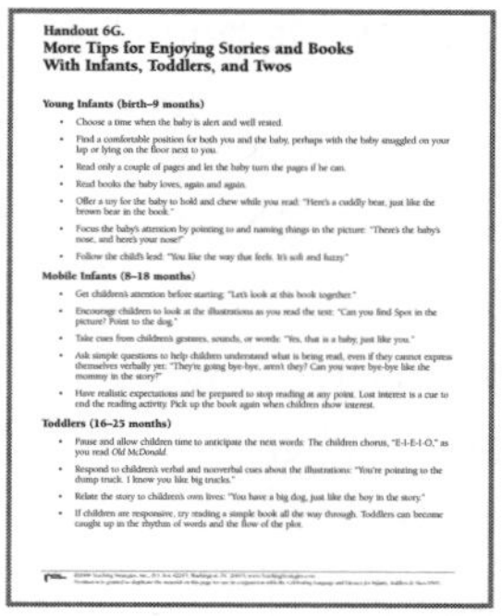

- ☐ Chart paper
- ☐ Markers
- ☐ Tape
- ☐ Books for infants, toddlers, and twos
- ☐ Handout 6D
- ☐ Handout 6E
- ☐ Handout 6F
- ☐ Handout 6G

Activity

Trainer's Note: If participants have already taken part in the "Viewing the Video: 'Enjoying Stories and Books'" workshop, begin the activity by asking them to share what they recall from the video. Ask if any of their book-reading practices have changed because of something they saw or heard in the workshop.

Tell participants that in the "Enjoying Stories and Books" video segment, one of the speakers includes selecting age-appropriate books in her list of ways to make book reading an interactive language experience.

Ask participants the following question:

- What do you look for when choosing books for infants, toddlers, and twos?

Write their responses on chart paper.

Possible responses:

Topics that are familiar to children
Beautiful pictures
Teach concepts such as color, shape, and size
Simple illustrations
Have things to feel and move, such as tabs, flaps, holes, and textures
Simple stories
Repetitive words or phrases
Words that rhyme
Humorous books

Tell participants they will now have a chance to look at some books and determine which are appropriate for infants, toddlers, and twos.

Distribute Handouts 6D, "Good Books for Infants, Toddlers, and Twos," and 6E, "Choosing Good Books for Infants, Toddlers, and Twos." Tell the participants to fill out Handout 6E by referring to Handout 6D.

Ask participants to share at their tables a book they looked at, and to talk about how they would use it to support children's language and literacy learning.

End the activity by sharing examples of your favorite books. Make the following points:

- Select high-quality books that you will enjoy sharing with children. Keep children's developmental abilities in mind and look for books that respect diversity and promote inclusion.

- Sharing books with young children helps them learn about themselves and others. Books help infants, toddlers, and twos identify and handle their emotions and feel connected to their families throughout the day.

- Looking at books encourages young children to use their fine motor skills as they reach, grasp, and hold books; put their fingers between pages; point to pictures; and turn pages.

- Books help children make sense of the world and learn new concepts. Young children get information and learn how to do many things from books.

- Book reading introduces children to the sounds and structures of language and helps them build vocabulary and increasingly complex language skills.

Distribute and briefly review Handout 6F, "General Tips for Reading and Storytelling With Children," and Handout 6G, "More Tips for Enjoying Stories and Books With Infants, Toddlers, and Twos."

Taking The Training Home

Invite participants to take the training home by doing the following:

- Use Handout 6D to review the collection of books in your room. Are your books appropriate for the children in your room? What, if any, changes do you need to make to your collection?

- Compare your book-reading practices with the practices on Handout 6F, "General Tips for Reading and Storytelling With Children," and Handout 6G, "More Tips for Enjoying Stories and Books With Infants, Toddlers, and Twos." Which strategies do you already use? Which ones, if any, have you not tried yet? Make sure you use good practices consistently, and try one of the practices you haven't tried yet.

Adapting the Workshop for Families

If you are presenting this workshop to families, consider the following adaptations:

- Use Handout F6D, "Good Books for Infants, Toddlers, and 2-Year Olds" as you select books for the table collections.

- As you introduce the workshop, include the following points in addition to infants' learning from books and the many places where children can look at books:

    Make books a regular part of home experiences and reading books a regular part of your everyday routines.

    You can enhance book reading by arranging comfortable places for your child to look at books—on his own and with you—and to hear them read aloud.

    You can always find high-quality children's books for free at the public library. When you provide good books for your child to touch, look at, and listen to, your child will grow to love books.

- Distribute and briefly review Handouts F6D, "Good Books for Infants, Toddlers, and 2-Year-Olds," and F6E, "Choosing Books for Your Infant, Toddler, or 2-Year-Old," in preparation for the book review activity.

- As you end the activity and share your favorite children's books, substitute the first point with the following:

    Choose good books that you will enjoy sharing with your child. Choose books that are about things she likes and things that interest her. Look for books that show children and families like yours and like the other children and families you know.

- In "Taking the Training Home," distribute Handout F6F, "Tips for Enjoying Stories and Books With Your Infant, Toddler, or 2-Year-Old" and suggest the following:

    Read and share books with your child daily.

    Handout F6F, "Tips for Enjoying Stories and Books With Your Infant, Toddler, or 2-Year-Old" has some good ideas for reading with your child. Some of these may be new ideas that you would like to try.

    If your child has several books, use the "Good Books for Infants, Toddler, and 2-Year-Olds" handout to evaluate the books and decide if they are the right ones for him.

    You can find great books for your child at the library. Bring the "Good Books for Infants, Toddlers, and 2-Year-Olds" handout to help you pick books for your child. You can also ask your early childhood program to set up a lending library for you and other families to use.

Handout 6D.
Choosing Books for Infants, Toddlers, and Twos

Directions: Choose one book to consider reading to children. Then answer the questions below.

Book Title: _____

Author: _____

What would children like about this book?

Is this book more appropriate for infants, toddlers, or twos? Why?

What could children learn through this book?

How does this book promote children's language and literacy skills?

Would you include this book in the collection of books in your room? Why or why not?

©2008 Teaching Strategies, Inc., P.O. Box 42243, Washington, DC 20015; www.TeachingStrategies.com
Permission is granted to duplicate the material on this page for use in conjunction with the *Celebrating Language and Literacy for Infants, Toddlers & Twos* DVD.

Handout 6E.
Good Books for Infants, Toddlers, and Twos

Young Infants (birth–9 months)

- Washable, sturdy, chewable books made of cloth, plastic, or vinyl

- Board books that are easily cleaned, with pages that are easy to turn

- Books with highly contrasting pictures, simple illustrations, or photos and with one or two objects on a page

- Books that have things to feel and move, such as tabs, flaps, holes, and a variety of textures

Mobile Infants (8–18 months)

- Sturdy books, such as board books

- Books with simple stories about babies, families, animals, and everyday experiences

- Books of songs, rhymes, and chants

- Simple stories with repetitive language

- Books with illustrations of familiar things that infants can point to or name

- Wordless books that picture familiar objects to name and count

Toddlers (16–25 months)

- Books that have simple plots and few words on each page

- Books about families and feelings, animals, and other everyday experiences such as saying "hello," "good-bye," and "goodnight"

- Books with pictures that introduce basic concepts about size, shape, and color

- Books with words and related illustrations placed closely together on the page

- Wordless books

- Alphabet books with simple, colorful illustrations

- Favorite stories, songs, or fingerplays toddlers can join in telling or acting out, such as "The Itsy Bitsy Spider"

- Books that make toddlers laugh

- Books that encourage toddlers to hunt for and point to hidden objects

Twos (24–36 months)

- Stories about them or children who are like them

- Books about animals

- Stories they can join in telling or act out, such as Eric Carle's *From Head to Toe*

- Books with rhymes, songs, chants, and other predictable language patterns

- Book versions of familiar songs such as "Old McDonald," "This Old Man," or "Row, Row, Row Your Boat"

- Books that show human diversity

- Books that help children think and talk about their own lives because they relate to their experiences, such as learning self-care skills0000000000000000, or to their fears, such as anxiety about separation, getting lost, or making a mistake

- Alphabet books with simple, familiar themes

- Books that have pictures with details that provide information about the characters and their activities

- Books that help children understand concepts about number, size, shape, and color

Handout 6F.
General Tips for Reading and Storytelling With Children

Become familiar with the book before you read it to the children. Think about what words might be new to the children so you can introduce them. Also think of questions you might ask about the pictures and the story.

Tell stories, as well as read them. The first time you read a story, talk or tell the story, rather than read it word for word. You can also tell stories by using wordless books and other storytelling props.

Make reading interactive. Set the stage. Snuggle. Build anticipation and excitement. Be a dramatic story reader, such as by pitching your voice high for Mama Bear and low for Papa Bear. Involve children in telling the story. Comment and wait for children to respond, ask questions and wait, and offer other prompts. Let children skip to their favorite pictures or pages. Encourage them to chant a book's repetitive phrases or fill in a missing rhyme. Point out when the story has ended, and ask whether they liked the story and whether they want to hear it again.

Follow the child's lead. Be ready to stop when the child loses interest. Watch for infants' cues. When young infants squirm, turn their head away, or push the book away, they are telling you that it is time to stop for now. Do not require children to sit during story time. While you are reading, allow children to crawl, toddle, or walk away and then return.

Be prepared to read the same story again and again. Children have favorites and do not tire of hearing those stories every day.

Link books to the daily routines in a child's life. If you are having difficulty calming a child for a nap, you might recite goodnight messages to some of the objects in your environment, just as in Margaret Wise Brown's *Goodnight Moon.* If you want to encourage children to dress themselves, you might repeat the advice given in Shigo Watanabe's *How Do I Put It On?*.

Handout 6G.
More Tips for Enjoying Stories and Books With Infants, Toddlers, and Twos

Young Infants (birth–9 months)

- Choose a time when the baby is alert and well rested.

- Find a comfortable position for both you and the baby, perhaps with the baby snuggled on your lap or lying on the floor next to you.

- Read only a couple of pages and let the baby turn the pages if he can.

- Read books the baby loves, again and again.

- Offer a toy for the baby to hold and chew while you read: "Here's a cuddly bear, just like the brown bear in the book."

- Focus the baby's attention by pointing to and naming things in the picture: "There's the baby's nose, and here's your nose!"

- Follow the child's lead: "You like the way that feels. It's soft and fuzzy."

Mobile Infants (8–18 months)

- Get children's attention before starting: "Let's look at this book together."

- Encourage children to look at the illustrations as you read the text: "Can you find Spot in the picture? Point to the dog."

- Take cues from children's gestures, sounds, or words: "Yes, that is a baby, just like you."

- Ask simple questions to help children understand what is being read, even if they cannot express themselves verbally yet: "They're going bye-bye, aren't they? Can you wave bye-bye like the mommy in the story?"

- Have realistic expectations and be prepared to stop reading at any point. Lost interest is a cue to end the reading activity. Pick up the book again when children show interest.

Toddlers (16–25 months)

- Pause and allow children time to anticipate the next words: The children chorus, "E-I-E-I-O," as you read *Old McDonald*.

- Respond to children's verbal and nonverbal cues about the illustrations: "You're pointing to the dump truck. I know you like big trucks."

- Relate the story to children's own lives: "You have a big dog, just like the boy in the story."

- If children are responsive, try reading a simple book all the way through. Toddlers can become caught up in the rhythm of words and the flow of the plot.

Handout 6G.
More Tips for Enjoying Stories and Books
With Infants, Toddlers, and Twos, continued

Twos

- Read books that have more extensive vocabularies than the children's speaking vocabularies.

- Most twos can sit and be a part of a small group of 2–4 children during a formal, but brief, story time. Remember to let children decide how long they want to stay with the group.

- Set the stage for story reading by talking about the book cover: "*The Snowy Day*, by Ezra Jack Keats. What do you see in this picture?"

- Help children focus their attention and begin to predict the story: "Poor Corduroy lost his button. I wonder where it is?"

- Encourage children to use the illustrations to understand and explain what is going on and to make predictions: "Where are the children now? What do you think will happen to the little girl now that it is raining?"

- Skip an expected phrase or part of a familiar story from time to time. Switch words or play with words in silly ways.

- After reading a story once through, ask questions while you read it again: "Do you remember what the caterpillar eats next?"

Handout F6D.
Good Books for Infants, Toddlers, and 2-Year-Olds

Young Infants (birth–9 months)

- Washable, sturdy, chewable books made of cloth, plastic, or vinyl

- Board books that are easily cleaned, with pages that are easy to turn

- Books with highly contrasting pictures, simple illustrations, or photos and with one or two objects on a page

- Books that have things to feel and move, such as tabs, flaps, holes, and a variety of textures

Mobile Infants (8–18 months)

- Sturdy books, such as board books

- Books with simple stories about babies, families, animals, and everyday experiences

- Books of songs, rhymes, and chants

- Simple stories with repetitive language

- Books with illustrations of familiar things that infants can point to or name

- Wordless books that picture familiar objects to name and count

Toddlers (16–25 months)

- Books that have simple plots and few words on each page

- Books about families and feelings, animals, and other everyday experiences such as saying *hello*, *good-bye*, and *goodnight*

- Books with pictures that introduce basic concepts about size, shape, and color

- Books with words and related illustrations placed closely together on the page

- Wordless books

- Alphabet books with simple, colorful illustrations

- Favorite stories, songs, or fingerplays toddlers can join in telling or acting out, such as "The Itsy Bitsy Spider"

- Books that make toddlers laugh

- Books that encourage toddlers to hunt for and point to hidden objects

Twos (24–36 months)

- Stories about them or children who are like them

- Books about animals

- Stories they can join in telling or act out, such as Eric Carle's *From Head to Toe*

- Books with rhymes, songs, chants, and other predictable language patterns

- Book versions of familiar songs such as "Old McDonald," "This Old Man," or "Row, Row, Row Your Boat"

- Books that show human diversity

- Books that help children think and talk about their own lives because they relate to their experiences, such as learning self-care skills, or to their fears, such as anxiety about separation, getting lost, or making a mistake

- Alphabet books with simple, familiar themes

- Books that have pictures with details that provide information about the characters and their activities

- Books that help children understand concepts about number, size, shape, and color

Handout F6E.
Choosing Books for Your Infant, Toddler, or 2-Year-Old

Directions: Choose one book to consider reading to your child. Then answer the questions below.

Book Title: _____

Author: _____

1. What would your child like about this book?

2. What could your child learn through this book?

3. How can you use this book to support your child's language and literacy skills?

Handout F6F.
Tips for Enjoying Stories and Books With Your Infant, Toddler, or 2-Year-Old

Young Infants (Birth-9 months)

- Choose a time when your baby is alert and well rested.

- Find a comfortable position for both you and your baby, perhaps with her snuggled on your lap or lying on the floor next to you.

- Read only a couple of pages and let your baby turn the pages if he can.

- Read books your baby loves again and again.

- Offer a toy for your baby to hold and chew while you read: "Here's a cuddly bear, just like the brown bear in the book."

- Focus your baby's attention by pointing to and naming things in the picture: "There's the baby's nose, and here's your nose!"

- Follow your child's lead: "You like the way that feels. It's soft and fuzzy."

Mobile Infants (8-18 months)

- Get your child's attention before starting: "Let's look at this book together."

- Encourage your child to look at the illustrations as you read the text: "Can you find Spot in the picture? Point to the dog."

- Take cues from your child's gestures, sounds, or words: "Yes, that is a baby, just like you."

- Ask simple questions to help your child understand what is being read, even if she cannot express herself verbally yet: "They're going bye-bye, aren't they? Can you wave bye-bye like the mommy in the story?"

- Have realistic expectations and be prepared to stop reading as soon as your child loses interest. Pick up the book again when he shows interest.

Toddlers (16-25 months)

- Pause and allow your child time to anticipate the next words: The child choruses, "E-I-E-I-O," as you read "Old McDonald."

- Respond to your child's verbal and nonverbal cues about the illustrations: "You're pointing to the dump truck. I know that you like big trucks."

- Relate the story to your child's life: "You have a big dog, just like the boy in the story."

- If your child is interested and ready, try reading a simple book all the way through. Toddlers can become caught up in the rhythm of words and the flow of the plot.

Two-Year-Olds

- Read books that have larger vocabularies than your child's speaking vocabulary.

- Set the stage for story reading by talking about the book cover: "*The Snowy Day*, by Ezra Jack Keats. What do you see in this picture?"

- Help your child focus her attention and begin to predict the story: "Poor Corduroy lost his button. I wonder where it is?"

- Encourage your child to use the illustrations to understand and explain what is going on and to make predictions: "Where are the children now? What do you think will happen to the little girl now that it is raining?"

- Skip an expected phrase or part of a familiar story from time to time. Switch words or play with words in silly ways.

- After reading a story once through, ask questions while you read it again: "Do you remember what the caterpillar eats next?"

WORKSHOP

Making a Book

- [ ] Chart paper
- [ ] Markers
- [ ] Tape
- [ ] Bookmaking materials
- [ ] DVD player and monitor, or computer and LCD projector
- [ ] *Strategies for Early Language and Literacy Development* video
- [ ] Handout 6H

Preparation

Gather the following bookmaking materials: zipper-lock plastic bags; construction paper, card stock or index cards that fit inside the plastic bags; hole punches; scissors; ribbon or yarn; magazines or catalogs with pictures (you may want to ask participants to bring these), and glue sticks or transparent tape.

You can provide one collection of materials for each table of participants or you can put sets of materials on display tables in the room and invite participants to get the materials they need and bring them back to their tables.

Cut construction paper or card stock to fit as pages inside the plastic bags. Rolling the paper slightly makes it easier to place in the bags.

Practice following the steps in Handout 6H, "Making Books for Children," so that you can easily demonstrate them.

Preview the "Enjoying Stories and Books" segment of the *Strategies for Early Language and Literacy Development* video.

Duplicate the handout.

Optional:

Review the following material in *The Creative Curriculum® for Infants, Toddlers & Twos*:

- "Enjoying Books and Stories," pages 115–117
- "What You Can Do and Say," page 120
- Chapter 13, "Enjoying Stories and Books," pages 323–340

Introduction

Introduce the workshop by making the following points:

- Book collections for infants, toddlers, and twos should include some homemade books.
- Homemade books are easy to make and can become some of children's most cherished items in your room.

Activity

Trainer's Note: If participants have already taken part in the "Choosing Books for Infants, Toddlers, and Twos" workshop, begin the activity by asking them to share their evaluations of their book collections and their book-reading practices. Ask whether and how their book-reading practices have changed since the workshop.

Show the "Enjoying Stories and Books" segment of the *Strategies for Early Language and Literacy Development* video. Tell participants to focus on the different kinds of homemade books they see in the video. Stop the video after all the examples are shown.

Ask participants what kinds of homemade books they saw in the video. Write their answers on chart paper. Ask why book collections for infants, toddlers, and twos should include some homemade books. As participants respond, make the following points:

- Young children, especially toddlers and twos, love to see pictures and hear stories about themselves and their families.

- Homemade books can help children connect home and your program.

- You can make many kinds of homemade books, including books filled with things to touch and smell and books about things such as the following:

    children and their families

    pets

    a child's day or routines

    a child's interests

    helping children deal with a fear or challenging issue

    a shared group experience

    simple objects and concepts

Ask participants to think about the interests and abilities of a particular child or those of children in a particular age-group in general. Invite them to make a homemade book that would interest that child or group of children.

Distribute Handout 6H, "Making Books for Children," and demonstrate the steps for making zipper-lock bag books. Allow time for participants to create their books. When they have finished, invite volunteers to share their books with the whole group.

End the activity by making the following points:

- You can make many kinds of homemade books for your collection.

- You can send homemade books home as gifts for families to share with their children.

Taking The Training Home

End the workshop by inviting participants to take the training home. Suggest that they try the following:

- Share the book you made with the children in your group. As you read the book, try these reading techniques:

    Focus children's attention by pointing to and naming things in the picture: "There's a circle. Tanya, Andre, and Oliver have circles on their shirts!"

    Take cues from children's gestures, sounds, or words: "Yes, that is an apple. I know that apple slices are your favorite snack."

    Ask simple questions about the pictures, even if children cannot express themselves verbally yet: "They're going bye-bye, aren't they? Can you wave bye-bye like the mommy in the picture?"

    Be prepared to stop looking at the book at any point. Lost interest is a cue to end the reading activity. Pick up the book again when children show interest.

- If you work with older toddlers or 2-year-olds, make books with the children.

- Share homemade books with families. Invite them to make their own books for and with their children.

Trainer's Note: You may also want to share Handout 6G, "More Tips for Enjoying Stories and Books With Infants, Toddlers, and Twos" with participants, especially if they have not participated in the "Choosing Books for Infants, Toddlers, and Twos" workshop.

Summary

If the participants have attended all three workshops in the "Enjoying Stories and Books" workshop series consecutively, summarize by making the following points:

- Read and tell stories to children every day.

- The words and pictures in books are important. Even more important is that your reading aloud and telling stories lets children know how much you value these activities.

- Children who learn to love language and books are more likely to become successful learners and lifelong readers.

Adapting the Workshop for Families

If you are presenting this workshop to families, consider the following adaptations:

- After participants have viewed the video and talked about the homemade books they saw, ask:

    Why do you think infants, toddlers, and 2-year-olds love homemade books?

- Distribute Handout F6G, "Making Books for Children," and demonstrate the bookmaking process.

- End the activity with the following points:

    You can make many kinds of books for and with your child.

    You can share your homemade books with your child's teachers as a way to help them get to know you and your child better.

- In "Taking the Training Home," add the following idea to the list of reading techniques:

    Follow your child's lead: "You're touching the bunny's fur. It's soft and fuzzy."

- You may also want to share Handout F6F, "Tips for Enjoying Stories and Books With Your Infant, Toddler, or 2-Year-Old" with the participants, especially if they have not participated in the "Choosing Books for Infants, Toddlers, and Twos" workshop.

Handout 6H.
Making Books for Children

Zipper-Lock Bag Books

1. Insert one page in each zipper-lock bag.

2. Punch two holes in the page, alongside the zipper.

3. Open the zipper and place pictures or other small items on the page. The items can be glued to the paper or left loose to move about.

4. Bind several pages together with ribbon or yarn.

5. Seal the plastic bags with tape or sew them closed to make the book permanent.

Variation: Instead of tying the pages together in book format, attach them together in a line.

Simple Picture Books

1. Take photos or cut out pictures of important objects in the children's lives. Digital cameras are excellent for taking photos. You can also ask families to send photos.

2. Paste the photos on cardboard or colored card stock.

3. Laminate the page or cover with clear Contact™ paper.

4. Punch holes in the pages and tie the book together with ribbon or yarn.

Variation 1: Make a "touch" book by pasting different textures of fabric on the pages.

Variation 2: Glue or tape Popsicle™ sticks to each page for a child who has difficulty turning pages.

Special Fun Book Ideas

Infants, toddlers and twos love books with holes, tabs, and other surprises. Make books with holes that babies can put their fingers through. For example, show a picture of a cup with a handle. Put a hole in the handle. String a number of these together, using the ideas above. Cover some of the pictures in your books with construction paper that children can open and shut to reveal the picture behind the paper. Paste a picture on a small brown bag (lunch size) so that children can open the folded end of the bag and see the rest of the picture. Surprise!

Handout F6G.
Making Books for Children

Zipper-Lock Bag Books

1. Insert one page in each zipper-lock bag.

2. Punch two holes in the page, alongside the zipper.

3. Open the zipper and place pictures or other small items on the page. (The items can be glued to the paper or left loose to move about.)

4. Bind several pages together with ribbon or yarn.

5. Seal the plastic bag with tape or sew them closed to make the book permanent.

Variation: Instead of tying the pages together in book format, attach them together in a line.

Simple picture books

1. Take photos or cut out pictures of important objects in your child's life.

2. Paste the photos on cardboard or colored card stock.

3. Laminate the page or cover with clear Contact™ paper.

4. Punch holes in the pages and tie the book together with ribbon or yarn.

Variation 1: Make a "touch" book by pasting different textures of fabric on the pages.

Variation 2: Glue or tape Popsicle™ sticks to each page if your child has difficulty turning pages.

Special Fun Book Ideas

Infants, toddlers, and 2-year-olds love books with holes, tabs, and other surprises. Make books with holes that babies can put their fingers through. For example, show a picture of a cup with a handle. Put a hole in the handle. String a number of these together, using the ideas above. Cover some of the pictures in your books with construction paper that your child can open and shut to reveal the picture behind the paper. Paste a picture on a small brown bag (lunch size) so that your child can open the folded end of the bag and see the rest of the picture. Surprise!